*To the memory of Albert, one of the good guys: respected for his honesty, loved for his warmth, admired for his love of life. A man who never stopped giving; a man who will be remembered for ever.*

Phillip Schofield – The Whole Amazing Story

Published by Robin McGibbon, Crystal Palace Park Road, London SE26 6UN.

Copyright © Robin McGibbon. April 12, 1992.

ISBN 0-9515938-11

Typeset and Printed by Status Graphics, Unit D, Broomsleigh Business Park, Worsley Bridge Road, London SE26 5BN

All rights reserved. No part of this publication may be reproduced, stored in a retrieval system or transmitted in any form, or by any means, electronic, mechanical, photocopying, recording or otherwise without the prior written permission of the publisher.

This book is sold subject to the condition it shall not, by way of trade or otherwise, be lent, resold, hired out or otherwise circulated without the publisher's prior consent in any form of binding or cover, other than that in which it is published and without a similar condition, including this condition being imposed on the subsequent purchaser.

All Shazam! photos: courtesy of TVNZ
Schofield family and Marika photos: Woman's Weekly (NZ).

# *THE AUTHORS*

The authors of this book are a father and son writing team, who have collaborated on two bestselling books: New Kids on the Block, The Whole Story, By Their Friends, which they published themselves; and Gazza! the first biography of the footballer, Paul Gascoigne, published by Penguin.

Robin McGibbon, 26, was a news reporter and showbusiness writer for several national newspapers before leaving in 1990 to write the New Kids book – a worldwide bestseller – and concentrate on full-time freelance writing. He lives in South London, near his mother, Toni, and sisters, Katrina, Alison and Jayne.

His father – also Robin – is a former national newspaper sub-editor and publisher, who began his book-writing career with Me and My Brothers, the life story of the Kray twins' brother, Charles. McGibbon then wrote For Ever and Ever Eamonn, the autobiography of the famous broadcaster and his wife, Grainne. McGibbon lives in Kent with his second wife, Sue, and two dogs – a labrador called Cassie, and Jock, a Scottie.

# OUR THANKS

Even with two of us working together on this tribute, we could not have completed it so swiftly without the help of so many people – from Newquay to New Zealand – who have known Phillip.

We must thank Phillip's teachers for their memories of the happy schoolboy; Ellen Gillis for her straight-talking; Ian Jago for stopping work; the Cannaford family for their hospitality; Sarah Strickland for giving us a laugh; and Louise Tucker for her personal photos. Thanks, also, to all those others in Newquay, who filled in important gaps, but who preferred not to be named.

The people of Auckland were fantastic and always willing to help, whether it was to grant a long interview or give directions to a lost and jet-lagged Pom. Particular thanks should go to Roger Beaumont at TVNZ; to Peter Grattan for changing his mind; to Miriam Tautz for being so open; and to Fritha Goodman for finding the time. On the business side, thanks to Budget Car for getting me on the road so smoothly.

Very special thanks indeed must go to Harold and Doreen Schofield, a warm, kind couple, for speaking with such honesty. We wish them much happiness in their new home.

Our thanks, also, to Ian Stubbs, in London, for making time while he was so busy with the General Election; to Paul Smith for helping trace people; and to Tim Mackay-Robinson for recalling Gordon's amusing infancy.

Extra special thanks must go to Chris Dagwell and Rob Phillips and their helpful and willing staff at Status Graphics for doing such a good job. And for ensuring the book was first.

On the personal side, thanks to Belinda Goldsmith for always staying in touch – a Chola for the North London boys, Simon Lee, Nick Esses and Ivor Davis and cheers to Micky Moynihan for always being in the right location!.

Above all, our heartfelt thanks to Sue for a very fine "Achievement" (!), both in the kitchen and in the study.

# *CONTENTS*

| | | |
|---|---|---|
| Chapter 1 | | Boy with a Dream |
| Chapter 2 | | Classroom Clown |
| Chapter 3 | | Torment in the Sun |
| Chapter 4 | | The Milky Bar Kids |
| Chapter 5 | | Close-Up On Romance |
| Chapter 6 | | Tears for a Friend |
| Chapter 7 | | Live, Dad, Live! |
| Chapter 8 | | Love Fades Away |
| Chapter 9 | | Farewell to Fame |
| Chapter 10 | | Gordon's First Squeak |
| Chapter 11 | | Sacked by the Boss! |
| Chapter 12 | | You're Brill, Phil |

Phillip, just 20, and on the threshold of stardom

Phillip's first home, 264 Heron Street, Oldham

This is the story of a boy with a dream – a boy who knew where he was going, and who refused to give up until he got there. It is a story of determination and grit, and the most overwhelming self-belief. It is about bouncing back from rejection and disappointment, and coping with tragedy and trauma. Above all, it is a story of success and the courage to battle against the odds to prove that, sometimes at least, a good guy *can* win.

The story starts in the Lancashire town of Oldham on April 1st 1962 – the day Patricia Schofield gave birth to a baby boy. Pat and her husband, Brian, had been happy in their terraced house, in Heron Street, but felt the grimy industrial town was not the ideal place to bring up their son. When the boy was 18 months, the couple moved to a pretty coastal resort in Cornwall, where they had spent their honeymoon. They loved the Cornish people as much as the fresh sea air, and could not think of a more idyllic place to live and raise a family.

The town was Newquay. And *that's* where the remarkable success story of their son, Phillip, really begins.

# 1

# Boy with a Dream

The little boy sat on his bed and switched on the tape recorder. For what seemed the hundredth time, he listened to the man speaking on the BBC.

The boy knew the words off by heart; he had written them down and read them silently to himself every time he played the tape. But it was not enough to know *what* to say. He had to learn *how* to say it. So he sat on his bed and listened carefully to the broadcaster's cultured tones, and the sedate speed of his delivery.

Later, the boy walked to a dressing table mirror and stood in front of it. He was a happy-go-lucky child, with an impish face, and he liked to laugh a lot. But the beaming smile that endeared him to his teachers and his family was not there now as he composed himself and said the words he knew so well. For speaking on radio was a very serious business, and the little boy could think of nothing he was more serious about than wanting to become somebody famous on the BBC.

It had been Phillip Schofield's ambition for as long as he could remember. Even at five, the radio held a special magic for him. And when his teacher at Trenance Infants School asked him what he wanted to be, Phillip didn't hesitate.

"A disc jockey," he piped up, brightly.

That teacher, Mrs Barbara Reeve, has sadly died, but her daughter, Jane, remembers her mother enthusing about Phillip.

"Most boys wanted to be a train driver or fireman, but Phillip was adamant he wanted to go on radio," Jane says. "Mum would always be talking about what a lively imagination he had, and how he'd walk around the school with a make-believe microphone in his hand, pretending to talk into it."

Barbie Reeve was a larger-than-life "theatrical" personality in Newquay, who produced shows for Newquay's Cosy Nook Theatre. And in Phillip – even at five – her showbusiness instinct detected a special sparkle that convinced her he was destined for stardom.

"Phillip was a super kid and definitely one of my mum's stars," Jane says. "He was not particularly clever, but he had a lively personality and loads of confidence that was surprising in one so young. He had a certain something that made him stand out from the other 30 kids in the class."

Barbie would enthuse about her "star" to teachers as well. One of them, Pauline Morris, an ancillary teacher, who helped out in what was called the Blue Room class, says: "Barbie was always talking about Phillip's special sparkle, and how he was going to be famous in something to do with showbusiness. Certainly I found him livelier and more confident than the average five or six-year-old, and always very quick with the answer back."

Not surprisingly, Phillip featured prominently in Barbie's school productions. And, today, 24 years later, another teacher, Mary Hatton, still remembers the first time she saw him.

"After being given a job at the school I was asked if I wanted to look around," she says. "There was a concert on in the assembly hall and the children were standing in lines. At the front, talking to Mrs Reeve, was this little boy with a big smile. She seemed to be consulting him, as opposed to telling him what to do, and it struck me that they got on well together.

"There was a band there and the boy may have been conducting it, or something. The other boys must have been less obvious for me to remember only Phillip. He was extrovert and confident – quite a character, even then. It was only a brief moment, but that smiling face, full of life, has stayed with me."

The infants' school, a short walk from the Schofields' new home at 17 St Thomas Road, seemed perfect too – until the day came for little Phillip to start there. Few five-year-olds relish the idea of leaving the family environment but Phillip positively hated it! The first day was all right: he went off, wearing his uniform proudly, and enjoyed himself. It was Day Two when the trouble started. Phillip threw a tantrum. He had been to school once, he wailed; he didn't see why he had to go again.

His mother explained that school was not just for one day, but every day – and little Phillip burst into tears, saying he wanted to stay with her. His mother had to force him out of the house and pull him along the road. Once inside the school building, she bundled him into the classroom and his teacher stood with her back against the door so that he could not run out.

It was like this for the first few days, and at playtimes Phillip would be so upset he would go off alone and sit under a tree in the school yard, waiting for his dad to walk past. At lunchtimes, he was taken home because he made other children cry.

A neighbour in St Thomas Road, Mrs Laura Varga, whose son, Timothy, was in Phillip's class, remembers Phillip's tears vividly.

"My earliest memory of him is a very tearful five-year-old," she says. "I'd be walking up the road with Tim and see Phillip's mum coaxing him along. He was crying and tugging on her arm, saying he didn't want to go. He'd still be crying when they got to the school, because he wanted to stay with his mum.

"I remember expecting Tim to miss me, and feeling deflated when he didn't. But Phillip was a very family-orientated child, who was always with his mum and dad, and it was obviously a huge shock for him to be apart from them.

"He did settle down, though, and was a pleasant lad, who mixed in with everyone. He was very tidily turned out with smart shirts

Phillip's second home, 17 St Thomas Road, Newquay

and shorts, and his hair was always neatly cut with short back and sides.

"Most small boys get into all sorts of mischief, and scuffles and end up with their shirt tails hanging out and mud on their knees. But I remember Phillip always being clean and tidy."

The following year, the Schofields sold their house in St Thomas Road and built a larger one in Lawton Close, Pentire, about a quarter of a mile from the seafront, as part of a four-family self-build group, which had council help. They turned the building into a guest house and converted the garage into an extra bedroom for the family so that they could accommodate more holidaymakers.

Pat and Brian worked hard together running the guest house and, during the day, Brian also used his crafting skills to make surf boards in a shop called Two Bare Feet.

It was the day after Guy Fawkes night that Phillip got involved in a skirmish that not only tarnished his 'clean and tidy' image, but also proved he had the guts to get tough if there was a point to prove.

It all began over a hunt for spent fireworks. Phillip had found a lot of duds and stacked them neatly in rows in a wheelbarrow. Four friends encountered him during his search and started teasing him, using his nickname of "Scabby," which they had given him a couple of years before. No one is quite sure how the name originated, but one of the four, Debbie Cannaford – now Teagle – thinks it was simply because it went so well with Schofield.

Debbie remembers that morning well. "We kept teasing Phillip: 'Nice fireworks you've got there, Scabby.' Suddenly the wheelbarrow went over. We started pinching his fireworks and Phillip went mad. He tried to grab some back off me, but I held on to them and before you knew it we were involved in an almighty fight on the ground, screaming and pulling each other's hair. I was older, but Phillip gave as good as he got and the fight was pretty 50–50.

"Finally, Phillip's mother, who was pregnant with Phillip's brother, Tim, heard the noise and came running out of her house into the garden. She pulled us apart and dragged Phillip home."

One of Debbie's friends, Ellen Gillis – now Agliano – who was there, wasn't the least surprised at Phillip's reaction. "Phillip was a horrible, spiky brat who was prone to throwing tantrums," she says.

"When his mother heard Phillip screaming she came flying down the street. If I'd been behaving like that, I'd have got a belt round the legs, but she was quiet and gentle, and concerned only at calming him down."

The Schofields' guest-house, at 8, Lawton Close

Anyone who is going to make it in showbusiness must have a tough, go-it-alone side to their nature. And even at seven and eight, when he was in junior school, Phillip was showing signs that he was not prepared to be one of the pack if it didn't suit him.

Ellen and Debbie and their brothers, Cernow and Gary, were still his friends, but he was not as close as the four of them. They were forever in and out of each other's houses, but Phillip rarely invited any of them home.

"He didn't really mingle," Ellen recalls. "He would join in some things, then keep to himself for a while. When he was part of the gang he was fine, and very funny, but when he wasn't, he seemed to go out of his way to spoil our fun.

"Once, we built a camp over the back of our gardens and painted it. We went indoors for lunch and came out to find someone had stuck grass on the wet paint. We knew it was Scabby."

Today, Ellen puts that down to Phillip's "spiteful" nature. But it seems it was more likely his weird sense of humour.

When Gary was four, Phillip made him drink something he said was lemonade, then admitted it was dogs' "pee". Whether it actually was, is questionable, but, to stick up for Gary, the others in the gang chased him with dogs' mess on the end of twigs.

Gary remembers Phillip's weird sense of humour at school, too. "He liked pretending he'd had a leg amputated. He'd bend his knee back so that his foot was inside his trousers, then hop around on the other leg. It was a strange thing to do, but it made us all laugh."

It is hardly surprising that a child who wanted to talk for a living should have been a chatterbox. And, according to Winsome Stoyle, who taught him in the third primary school year at Newquay Juniors, he was in a class of his own.

"He never seemed to stop," she remembers. "I tried to shut him up once. But it was a losing battle. I said: 'Phillip do you *ever* stop talking?' He just shrugged his shoulders and grinned. As a teacher, you can only relate yourself to the child and say: 'Come on, get on with it.' If he talked too much and didn't do his work, he would have to stay in and do it during playtime. In the end, he did quieten down a bit, but I do remember having to keep him in several times.

"He was a most interesting child, though, and easy to talk to.

One of my lasting memories of him is his handwriting. It was terrible – very spidery and difficult to read.

"I tried hard to improve it, but he had such a fast mind it went far quicker than the written word. He knew the answers to questions but was always too quick putting his thoughts on paper to really concentrate on his actual writing. That sums him up, really. He was so lively, he never gave himself time to knuckle down and present a nice piece of work; any-old-how would do.

"But he had writing talent – there's no doubt about that. In his time with me, a monthly magazine called Child Education ran a competition in which pupils had to write the ending to an adventure story involving children trapped in space. Phillip's was so good, I sent it in – with a few others – and he won a book token on behalf of the school. The story was only about 150 words long, but it had a novel twist to it and was definitely the best in the class. The book Phillip won is still in the school library.

"I took music, but did not find Phillip outstanding in any way. He never showed particular flair and I don't remember him trying to sing."

Phillip's teacher in the fourth year was Reginald Buscombe, an old-fashioned strict teacher, who achieved local fame when he was chosen as a linesman for the famous "Stanley Matthews" Cup Final between Blackpool and Bolton Wanderers in 1953.

Most children were scared of Mr Buscombe, but not Phillip: he would take all his shouting with a smile and not let it bother him. He would go up to another teacher, Joyce Cane, in the playground and say: "Mister Buscombe's in a a bad mood today. Oh, well, never mind." Then he'd go off and play, not bothered in the least.

Another teacher, Eric Rabjohn, describes Phillip as one of those children a teacher doesn't forget.

"A lot of children you wouldn't recognise from Adam, but you would always notice that Phillip was around. He was a memorable person – a lively, likeable rogue. You couldn't ignore him.

"I was taking sport then, but Phillip was not into games. He didn't sparkle, certainly never won anything. I don't remember him on the football field, but if he was, he'd be one of the talkers who wouldn't want the ball to come anywhere near him.

"He wasn't naughty, but could be a bit of a nuisance at times. I had to tell him off once for playing in the long jump pit at the senior school. The pits were sacrosanct – even the teachers weren't allowed to touch them. But on this particular day, Phillip and some other boys were in the pits, using the sand for some game or other. If Mr Buscombe had seen them there'd have been hell to pay, so I gave them a good ticking off and told them to get out. Phillip responded well."

Phillip always had the latest toys. He was the first of his friends to have a walkie-talkie, a Joe 90 secret agent kit in a plastic suitcase, and he even had a pair of stilts. He was not a spoiled boy, however. His parents bought him toys, of course, but, by now, Phillip was waiting on tables in their guest house and getting paid for it. In the evenings, he helped his dad in the Two Bare Feet, keeping his homework under the counter and catching up on it when business was slow.

"He put what he earned in a jar," says Debbie Teagle. "He never wasted money. He'd save up so that he could have the latest toys, and he looked after everything he bought."

As he neared his tenth birthday, there was something Phillip wanted more than anything – a disc jockey disco set. And when he got it, there was no prouder kid in the whole of Newquay. For once, he was keen to invite Ellen and Debbie and the rest of the gang into his home. Glowing with pride, he showed them into the dining room, then sat behind the disco set to show them how it worked.

"The set had the full biz – turntable, flashing lights, the lot," Ellen recalls. "I can't remember Phillip telling us he wanted to go on radio, but I suppose it must have been obvious, because he loved that disco so much. Sometimes we'd see the lights flashing and hear the music throughout the day.

"To us, though, it was funny. Looking back, we seem to have spent a lot of time finding Phillip funny and laughing at him."

What they would have found even more laughable, had they known, was Phillip's ambitious plan to work for the BBC. Even then, at ten, he was writing to Broadcasting House with lots of questions – and using a typewriter so that the people who read his letters wouldn't know how old he was.

Now that, Ellen and Co. *would* have found very funny.

To teachers, however, Phillip was far from a figure of fun. He was a conscientious, helpful and lively boy – a joy to have in the class. He was a very good-looking lad, too, and when the 1972 pantomime season approached and the school started holding auditions for a Cosy Nook production of Cinderella, they knew they did not have to look far for the perfect Prince Charming.

In the event, Phillip was not a clear-cut favourite. He had appeared in only minor roles in previous shows, including his debut as a mouse, then as a schoolchild in a crowd scene in Red Riding Hood the year before. There were two other candidates with, arguably, more natural acting talent: Conrad Flynn and Simon Martin. Auditions were held at lunchtimes in September. Several other children were put forward by their teachers for the Prince Charming role, but the show's producer, Hilda Folland, knew early on that it was between Phillip, Conrad and Simon.

"Most of the children didn't take the audition seriously, but Phillip lapped it up," she says. "He had a tremendous personality, even then. He loved being up on the stage. And when he said a few lines, my co-producer Reg Moss and I knew he was going to get the part.

"When he spoke, it was as if he believed he really was the Prince. He was nice-looking, too, with an adorable cheeky grin and, to be honest, we picked him for looks as well as his personality.

"I can't remember his reaction when he learned he'd been chosen for the part; the roles were probably announced on the school notice board and I wouldn't have been there to see him. But, knowing Phillip, he would have just beamed. That was his reaction to most things.

"As you can imagine, rehearsals were fun. Phillip could be a wag when he wanted, but Conrad and Simon, who were cast as The Ugly Sisters, were the real live wires and were always up to something, trying to get some laughs.

"For kids so young, they had tremendous timing and were very funny. The minute Phillip started saying his lines, they'd be right at the front, in the footlights, pulling their large, padded bras around and ad-libbing, trying to raise a laugh.

"Phillip took it all very well. After all, there wasn't much for him to say. He just had to look nice – which he did.

"He was particularly pleased to get the Prince Charming role because he got to kiss Cinderella, who was played by a lovely girl, named Louise Tucker, who was popular with the boys.

"When I told Phillip in rehearsal that he must kiss Louise, he gave me the familiar grin and shrugged his shoulders, pretending he wasn't bothered. But I'm sure he loved the idea of kissing Louise – any of the boys would have wished they could. It was only a peck on the cheek, but the boys were only ten, after all."

To kiss pretty Louise was certainly a bonus for Phillip, but, more importantly, it meant he had a great reason for seeing her outside school. She only lived round the corner, and now they were going to be young stage stars, she had to go to his house a couple of evenings a week to prepare for their big opening night. They were only ten, but they were taking their forthcoming moment of fame very seriously.

Louise's older sister, Nici, went to the private rehearsals because she was in the panto, too. She was to be Louise's stand-in when Cinderella's rags are turned into a glittering ballgown. As the Fairy Godmother casts her spell, the theatre lights go out and the sisters quickly switch places. As far as the audience would be concerned, Louise had miraculously changed into a stunning princess, but while Nici was on stage, Louise would be changing into an identical outfit for the next scene.

Rehearsals at Phillip's house took place in a sparsely-furnished back room with a wooden floor. There, he and Louise learned how to waltz for the show's classic ballroom scene, where Cinderella meets her Prince Charming.

"The room was perfect for us because it was so bare," Louise recalls. "We would get dressed up in full costume – make-up and everything. Phillip had to wear blue eyeshadow, which we laughed about. When I was younger, I'd had ballet classes, so I had a fair idea how to dance. But Phillip had two left feet and had no idea. He took it quite seriously and tried very hard to learn, though. Phillip's mum and dad watched us and we had a lot of fun. In fact, we spent most of the time practising that dance and our singing, rather than learning our lines.

"Supposedly, some boys liked me at school, but I had no idea then. Certainly I didn't know Phillip liked me in any special way."

By the opening night, Thursday, December 7, the two children's hard work had paid off. Instead of feeling terrified, as you would expect, they were oozing confidence – particularly Phillip.

Hilda Folland remembers: "When we opened, I can clearly remember Phillip totally calm. I went from the wings, through a sound proof door into a narrow corridor where the 180 children in the cast were waiting, amid all kinds of bedlam.

"'Schofield,' I called. 'Quick now. Hurry up.'

"And Phillip strolled up, grinning cheekily: he'd evidently been fooling around. He wasn't the slightest bit on edge. He was loving it.

"He was wearing a brocade blue jacket, with satin trimming, knee-length breeches, white socks and black shoes with gilt edges. His mum had added bits of gold to give the outfit a little sparkle. He had a white cotton wool, Regency-style wig with big curls, tied in a bow at the back. Typically, he had pulled the wig to the back of his head so that his own hair showed at the front.

"He sidled up to me and put his hands on his hips. 'Oh, Miss Folland,' he said, very theatrically. He was always a bit cheeky, and I couldn't help smiling.

"'Stand still, Schofield,' I said and pulled the wig straight.

"He wasn't in my class so he didn't know me at all well. But he was perfectly at ease with me. And he was as cool as you like, performing on stage.

"Some people have said he was shy and retiring at school, but that's not the Phillip I remember. There are so many children a teacher forgets. Phillip isn't one of them.

"Each of the three shows went extremely well and ended with a grand finale, all 180 children on stage together. A little gap was left for Phillip and Louise to come through, hand in hand, to take their bow in the centre of the stage.

"Reaching the front, Phillip made a flourishing and extravagant bow. There were three or four curtain calls and lots of cheering from 500 children and parents in the audience. Phillip stood on that stage, grinning like the Cheshire cat, lapping it up."

It was a great night for Louise, too. But, sadly, the kiss that was so important to Phillip was not so exciting for her.

Today, she says: "I can't really remember it at all, I'm sorry to say. My one vivid memory of the performance was Phillip and I singing You'll Never Walk Alone after the Prince had found Cinderella and she had tried on the slipper. We stood on the right of the stage and sang to one another.

"It was a very moving song and whenever I hear it now I think of us on stage together. I remember Phillip having a reasonable voice even then.

"Cinderella and the Prince were the two main stars and we got standing ovations every night. The last night was particularly good, really powerful. When we took our bow, it was fantastic. But when you're just ten, you don't see it as adulation – it's just exciting."

It is evident that, even then, Phillip was aware of his appeal. Even if he hadn't captured Louise Tucker's heart.

And it is clear, too, that in the five years since starting school, his ambition had not wavered: he was still determined to be a radio broadcaster.

Joyce Cane, who was involved in rehearsals, remembers him telling her so – with a confidence she has never forgotten.

She says: "One night, backstage, Phillip was changing into his white wedding costume when he turned to me and said: 'One day, I'm going to be famous, you know.'

"You'd expect lots of kids to say, 'I'm going to be a doctor or something' and you'd not be the slightest bit convinced they would achieve what they said, even if they meant it.

"But Phillip had a certain conviction that struck me. I can't put my finger on why. I think it was just that, even then, he had that added sparkle, that little bit of confidence the other kids didn't.

"I remember thinking: 'I bet you *will* be, too."

# 2

# Classroom Clown

It was Monday, July 23, 1973. It was blistering hot. And Newquay was at fever pitch. The BBC's first Radio One Roadshow was coming to town.

The show was the brainchild of Johnny Beerling, then a top producer at Radio One. On a camping holiday in France, he'd seen a radio show taken out of the studio and staged in the open air in front of thousands of pop fans. Stunned by the response, he thought: If it can work here, it can work in Britain.

Back in his Broadcasting House office, a few weeks later, he contacted a friend in the motor trade and asked him to make a mobile stage, big enough for recording equipment necessary for an outside broadcast.

Bristol-based businessman John Miles and his brother, Tony, made what was, in effect, a wooden stage inside an 18-feet box, able to be towed by another car or van. And, towards the end of July, the wheels of the revolutionary Roadshow were ready to roll.

Newquay, one of Britain's most popular resorts, was chosen as the venue, and veteran Alan Freeman as the disc jockey to host the show. Details were plugged over and over again on the air and colourful circus-style posters put up on walls and in shops throughout Newquay.

The two-hour show, locals and holidaymakers were informed, would start at 5 p.m. on the sands of Fistral Bay, a beautiful stretch of beach where the World Surfing Championships were sometimes held.

## CLASSROOM CLOWN

No one knew what to expect – not even the BBC and the man behind the show. They knew what music they were going to play and who would be at the turntables. But they hadn't a clue how many people would turn up. It might be a handful. It could be 20,000.

If Beerling and Co. had been in Newquay the day before that memorable Monday, however, they would have known they had a success on their hands. The place was buzzing with Roadshow talk. Young pop fans – locals and holidaymakers alike – were beside themselves with excitement.

None more so than Phillip.

To an 11-year-old who yearned to be a disc jockey, the show was more than he could ever have wished for. For six years, he had been fascinated, enchanted and bewitched by the wonder of radio without knowing, for sure, how the magic worked. Now, he would be able to see what he'd only been able to hear. What had existed only in his imagination would be there in front of his eyes.

It is unlikely any kid in Newquay that Sunday was wishing away the hours to Monday more than Phillip. Whether his excitement kept him awake that night is not known. What is certain is that he was one of the first children on Fistral beach the next morning when Alan Freeman and his BBC team arrived.

Enthralled, Phillip sat on the sand dunes with hundreds of other schoolkids, watching the Miles brothers turn their travelling box into a stage. And, at 5 p.m., when the Roadshow went on air for the first time, he was sitting on the sand in the front row, just ten feet from the stage, as if in a trance.

For two fun-filled, noisy hours that memorable Monday evening, Phillip was swept along joyously on a wave of mass hysteria and personal euphoria. It was a marvellously magical time – arguably the most wonderful time of Phillip's young life.

Not for one moment did the extrovert side of his personality prompt him to get up on that stage; he just sat and listened and watched, mesmerised by all the equipment and captivated by the sparkling spontaneity of it all.

And when it was all over and he and his pals walked from the beach, with their autographs and their memories, his mind was alive with all the possibilities his future could hold. He had seen a real-life BBC disc jockey at work – and he had loved what he'd seen. It was everything he thought. And more.

That September, when he started at Tretherras Senior School, the flame of his broadcasting ambition, already burning brightly, had exploded into a roaring fire.

Within two years at Tretherras, Phillip had established himself as something of a hero among his classmates because of his entertainment value. As a primary school child, he had been a live-wire and full of fun. Everyone knew him as Scabby by now and, at 13, he was outrageous and often downright naughty. The rest of the class would look to him to mess around and cause a disruption – and Phillip rarely let them down.

One close friend, Sarah Strickland, who sat near him in Maths, says: "Scabby was definitely the instigator of any mischief. He'd encourage us all to muck around and generally cause havoc. He was particularly naughty in maths, because all our teachers were walk-overs and let us get away with all sorts of things.

"As soon as they turned their backs to write on the blackboard, Scabby would start snorting like a pig or miaowing like a cat or make loud farting sounds. Other times he'd throw bits of paper at the board. The teacher would turn round and know immediately who was responsible, even though Scabby was sitting in the back row, with his head down. The teacher would tut and tell him not to be stupid, and Scabby would sit there, not looking up, just shaking with laughter. He'd be quiet for a few minutes, then start acting up again. His pranks were terribly juvenile, but he found them hilarious. We did, too, because we were all bored with maths and it lightened the whole thing up."

Once, however, Phillip pushed his luck too far. He and a pal, Gary Moyse, messed around so much that, after several warnings, their teacher cracked. He ordered both boys to leave their desks at the back of the class and sit at the front where he could keep an eye on them. Phillip, who liked disrupting the class in an "undercover" sort of way, without getting caught, was acutely embarrassed – and showed it.

"He went bright red," Sarah recalls. "Normally he got away with things by just smiling and being charming, but this time, it didn't work and he was made to feel foolish. It didn't stop him, however. When the teacher's back was turned, he and Gary sent messages to me and another girl on paper darts and a rubber."

When Phillip was 14, perhaps 15, he overstepped the mark with a young French teacher, and regretted it. The teacher was very prim and wore long Laura Ashley-style dresses. She was so soft the class ran rings round her.

Sarah recalls: "One day, we had French as the first subject in the afternoon. It was obvious Scabby and Gary had been up to something during the lunch break, because they were all secretive and giggling as we sat at our desks."

The class found out what it was immediately the teacher folded back the blackboard. There, stuck down with sellotape, was an explicit colour photograph of a naked girl, from the centre pages of a sex magazine. The teacher was so embarrassed and distressed, she ran out of the room in tears.

"The classroom was bedlam," says Sarah. "Scabby and Gary were rolling around, laughing their heads off, and, to be honest, the rest of us thought it funny, too – at first. But, then, we started feeling bad because the teacher had been so upset. We told Scabby and Gary that they'd gone too far. Scabby was never a malicious child, and would not have wanted to cause the teacher distress; it was just his wicked sense of humour. He loved to have fun and I'm sure he expected her to see the funny side."

It was Phillip's "wicked sense of humour" that made him pleased to be part of The Jobbies, a make-believe club, consisting of four members: himself, Sarah, Gary and another girl named Jackie.

Sarah recalls: "To us, a pooh was a Jobby and when anyone ever said anything about a job, we'd crack up. We would write songs and poetry about Jobbies and pretend we were all members of The Jobbies Club. Scabby would come to school with a plastic Jobby, and put it down in the playground. We'd stand around in a group and laugh as other kids gave it a wide birth, thinking it was real. We all thought it hilarious.

"I got on well with Scabby. Most boys in their early or mid teens made crude or nasty comments about girls' chests, but not him. He was interested in girls only as friends and got on well with them. All the other boys teased me about being flat-chested, but not Scabby. He never mentioned it once."

Homework, it seems, was something Phillip was reluctant to do. Whether he was too busy writing letters to the BBC, helping his dad in the surf-board shop or brushing up his disco technique is not clear. Certainly he admitted to his pals that he'd lain awake in bed until midnight, listening to all the latest American sounds on Radio Luxembourg, the only commercial station at the time. And he would turn up at school with his homework not done, begging his friends to help him out.

Says Sarah: "He'd come into the classroom well before the lesson was due to start and say: 'Have you done that homework yet? Oh, let me copy it please.' He wasn't stupid or anything – he just didn't seem to be bothered or worried about not doing it. One of us always let him have a look at what we'd done.

"It was the same when it came to monthly tests for the streaming system. Neither he nor Gary bothered to revise; instead Scabby would lean over and copy from me or Jackie, then lean the other way so Gary could copy off him."

Whether Phillip would have achieved more had he worked more and mucked around less is debatable. By no means was he dim; but he was not especially bright either, and it is questionable whether he had the ability and application to reach spectacular academic heights. What is certain is that, at 14, the same single-mindedness he had shown towards ambition at ten – and, perhaps, five – was burning as fiercely as ever. It was as if school was a tedious and time-consuming obstacle he had to overcome before he could get on with what was really important in his life. The teachers at Tretherras Seniors may not have been overly impressed with his classroom performance, but they could hardly fault his live-wire personality, his good manners or charm.

And they could not fail to admire his determination.

His English teacher, Gerry Green, who was also a careers adviser, cannot remember another boy so adamant about what he was going to do when he left school; and so convinced he would achieve it. For the first time in her career, she was stonewalled: no matter how much she tried to persuade Phillip to consider alternative careers to broadcasting, she could not sway him.

"I came up against a brick wall," she recalls, smiling. "I had no chance. Phillip knew what he was going to do and nothing I said made the slightest difference.

"I'd just seen a boy who said he wanted to be a rock guitarist and when Phillip said he wanted to interview famous people for the BBC, I thought, 'Oh, God, not another one with wild ideas.'

"'Yes, Phillip,' I said, rather patronisingly. 'Very nice, Phillip. Now, if you couldn't do that, what else would you like to do?'

"'I don't want to do anything else,' Phillip replied.

"I thought, I can't be cruel to the lad, so I started talking about other possible careers, such as computers. I pushed it and pushed it for 10 minutes or so, but Phillip was immovable. Be sensible, I said – there must be something else you fancy doing apart from working for the BBC. But he just shook his head. 'That's all I've ever wanted to do,' he said.

"I was impressed with his singlemindedness, but, in all honesty, I thought his ambitions were totally unrealistic. He was the typical 14-year-old, with blushes and spots. And, with his glasses, he was hardly prepossessing.

"I would love to say I saw he had charisma. But I didn't. There was nothing to indicate he was the type to draw the best out of people.

"When I came to fill in Phillip's careers' form, I didn't know what to put down. I don't think I filled in anything, because I'd come up against a brick wall. I can't recall if he said anything at the end of our chat, but he was a polite lad and he probably tried to pacify me.

"I put his wild ambition down to adolescent dreaming: I thought he'd just have to live and learn. Certainly it never crossed my mind that he would, indeed, go on and interview people."

What would not have crossed Gerry Green's mind, either, is that, once at home, alone with his dreams, Phillip continued typing out letters to the BBC and anyone else who might be interested in a young kid with broadcasting ambitions. Gerry Green's scepticism, if not her downright disbelief in him, would have registered, because Phillip was a listener. But it would have done nothing to soften his resolve, dampen his determination. Breaking into broadcasting would be hard; he had the intelligence and vision to accept that. But he had a quality which, coupled with his singlemindedness, could be the difference between success and failure: self-belief.

That's why Gerry Green had found him a brickwall. And why the letters would continue to go out until he got a positive reply.

At that time, sadly, the replies from the BBC's management were far from positive. They were polite enough, but hardly encouraging or inspiring. Phillip even wrote to disc jockeys, but only one bothered to reply. She was Anne Nightingale, a Brighton-based disc jockey, who'd made national headlines in the sixties by becoming the BBC's first woman record spinner. Anne did offer encouragement, but warned: You'll find it tough. Phillip treasured her personal reply. It was a gesture he would never forget.

The odds against Phillip making it were very high. He knew that, but they didn't bother him. In fact, according to teacher Bruce Connock, he relished them.

Mr Connock, who taught the fifth form, admits: "I told Phillip that getting into the BBC was a pipedream – he wouldn't do it even if he stayed at school until he was 90!

"It wasn't like wanting to be a hairdresser or builder, or even a teacher. One would say, 'Okay, this is the route, off you go.' But broadcasting was different; the odds against succeeding were so high. I compared him to another pupil, Chris Morris, who wanted to be a pro footballer. We told him he was unlikely to make a living from the game and to make sure he had academic qualifications. In the event, Chris played for Celtic and Ireland in the World Cup, but he kept his options open right up to A-level, and he had a college place as well.

"Phillip accepted that the odds against getting into the BBC were high, but I would have said he rather liked them. He told me: 'I know it's going to be difficult, but radio is what I really want to do and I'm going to give it my best shot.' I got the impression that the BBC was something he believed in and he was going to get there no matter what he had to do. It was as simple as that.

"The Phillip I remember is a very happy, cheerful, extrovert or perhaps a bit zany – who listened to what I had to say, and concentrated on what he had to do, with a big smile on his face the whole time.

"He was never a problem with other lads; he related well and very easily to everybody. He was a thoroughly nice, outgoing lad, with a genuine interest in people, and a desire to help them. I never saw him as a joker, getting up to daft pranks; to me, he was always clean, tidy, well-mannered, pretty sensible, very co-operative and doing all the things you hope an average teenager would."

Other teachers, too, were still dubious about broadcasting as his sole career hope: despite his unwavering resolution, few of them, it seems, took him totally seriously; most urged him to put broadcasting out of his mind and consider alternatives.

And then Phillip had an impromptu, casual chat with his tutor, Jill Stanley. And, for once, he got some positive feed-back, not the customary: "You must be mad – think of something else."

Jill, who took Phillip and nine or ten other pupils for general studies, suggested alternative careers, because she always did. But she listened to what he'd been doing to try to interest the BBC in him and was impressed. Behind the uninhibited smile and fun-loving, zany personality, Jill detected a fierce dedication, a quiet bloody-mindedness, that made her think: if anyone is going to do what they say, you are.

Today, Jill recalls: "We had a very pleasant lesson, just sitting talking, putting the world to rights, and Phillip happened to stay behind after the bell went. I asked what he was going to do and he told me he'd been writing to the BBC, and other organisations, for years about a job. I suggested some alternatives, but I was pleased and not a little surprised at the lengths he'd gone to and told him he was doing the right things.

"I usually tell youngsters how to go about breaking into something, how they've got to be prepared to sit on people's doorsteps, as it were. But I didn't have to say that to Phillip, because he'd done it already. I did warn him that journalism was a very tough business to get into, but he didn't seem in the least put off.

"He was obviously dedicated. It wasn't overtly noticeable – more of a quiet perseverance.

"Phillip was a very self-possessed polite young man. Unlike a number of teenagers, who talk in grunts, he was very easy to talk to. With all that, plus his determination and sheer effort, I didn't think: Hey, you won't make it in a million years. I genuinely felt that his doggedness and commitment might just get him there.

"I can't remember exactly, but the chances are that, at the end of our little chat, I would have said: 'Good luck to you if you do make it."

In the run-up to his mock O-levels, early in 1978, and the real thing that June, Phillip did get his head down. He wasn't going to take A-levels, but he saw the advantage of getting as many O-level passes as possible.

Outside school, however, revision – like previous homework – did not seem to be a top priority. Instead, he set himself up as a one-boy disc jockey service, running discos at hotels in the Newquay area. He even splashed out on business cards which said

SUPER SOUNDS FROM THE GALAXY DISCO. In the bottom left-hand corner they had his name, Phil Schofield. In the right was his phone number: Newquay 4807. Phillip proudly distributed them around town to potential clients. Any money he earned, he ploughed back into the business by buying the latest pop records, to add to his ever-growing collection.

Those early discos were not wild dance nights for young people as you would expect a budding young DJ to run, because Phillip's first party-goers were nearly all over 50. Phillip didn't mind. He just thought of the valuable experience he was gaining, speaking in public and learning to become a disc jockey for a real audience, not just his family in the dining room.

The disco business grew and grew. And the more he did, the more confident he became. Soon, Phillip was looking for a new challenge and a wider audience. What he needed was a proper radio situation. Hospital radio presented the perfect answer and he immediately typed a letter to the main hospital in Truro, a large town nearly 40 miles from Newquay, which he knew ran its own station. But he got a loud No. At 15, he was too young, they said. Hospital policy could not be dodged, no matter how keen he was.

Phillip was not unfamiliar with letters of rejection. He refused to be upset by the disappointment and, instead, simply looked for the next reasonable option. He chose Plymouth Hospital Radio, and two weeks after his 16th birthday, he wrote to its controller asking for a job. This time he wasn't too young and, at his interview, impressed the radio bosses with his confidence and knowledge of music enough to land a weekend job.

It was a major break and the first real step to fulfilling the radio dream he had had for so many years. It was far from ideal, however. Phillip wasn't getting paid, because he was hired purely on a voluntary level, and the radio base – at Lockyer Street Hospital in Plymouth – was an expensive two-hour train journey from Newquay.

But, at last, he had his own radio show – with an audience of more than 2,000 patients in six hospitals scattered over the city. He decided to call it Phillip Schofield's Bran Tub.

Each Saturday, Phillip set off from Newquay to work and learn and entertain those patients. Back home, he left his friends and classmates to relax and enjoy the things most teenagers do on a Saturday.

One of them Ian Jago, says: "None of us should have been surprised at his dedication, because Phillip was the most out-going of all of us. He told us he was convinced he was going to be famous on radio, and we would laugh because it sounded so silly that any of us could be that lucky. We saw our lives being built in Newquay and didn't think much beyond that. Our laughing didn't bother Phillip in the least, not only because we were *always* laughing at each other, but because he knew that was what he really wanted to do, and it didn't matter one bit to him what we thought.

"Nearly all his money seemed to go on records. He'd buy a new one every weekend and tell us all about it at school on the Monday.

"He seemed to get on with everyone. In our form, he was definitely one of the more popular boys with the girls, and he got on well with all the teachers, too. He was good fun, always happy-go-lucky and cheery. Nothing ever seemed to get to him. Nothing ever fazed him.

"He was very conscientious and always did well in English Literature. He would read from our set books very confidently, but he wasn't what you would call a big-head. He didn't always have his hand up wanting to read because he knew how good he was.

"Phillip wasn't a sporty type and didn't enjoy games or athletics. Cross country running was a big event, but not for Phillip and I, and his two best mates, Gary Moyse and Martin Edmonds.

"We were supposed to run four miles round the local area, but hit on a great way to save our energy. Gary lived on the route and the four of us would stop off there for a drink, courtesy of Gary's mum. We'd wait for the others to come past, on their way back to school, and tag on the end. If any other kids tumbled what we were doing, no one ever told on us."

Like many of his schoolmates, Ian remembers Phillip as a

prankster. And once the O-levels were over and the pressure off, he was getting up to all sorts of harmless fun – anything that would raise a laugh.

Towards the end of term, Phillip, Ian and three other pupils went back to school in the evenings to do some scene shifting for a production of Tom Sawyer. On the last night, they decided to play a joke on Sarah Ricard, a student teacher not much older than themselves.

"We waited for her to come backstage, then pounced on her," says Ian. "Phillip got her in a head lock and held her still while another boy and I painted her face with make-up sticks. Phillip was tall for his age and she was little, so he didn't have any trouble keeping her still. We all got on well with her – particularly Phillip – and knew we could get away with it. Phillip thought it was a great prank. And she had a good laugh, too."

That summer the laughing stopped. His O-levels were over and Phillip had to think hard about his future. He had carried on writing to the BBC, but was no nearer to getting a job. He'd told them about his work on Plymouth Hospital Radio but they were not impressed. When he learned he had got some good O-level passes, he told them about that, too. But they still did not give him the job he craved. Phillip resigned himself to staying at school for another year in the lower sixth. He decided to re-take the maths O-level he had failed, and took a typing and secretarial course which he felt would help his BBC chances.

At weekends, he continued his hospital radio show and his Newquay disco business. He was getting more and more proficient – and confident.

At this time, Phillip's parents, particularly his mother, were tired of running the guest house, so they decided to sell their home in Lawton Close and build a cottage on a plot of land near the beach in Crantock, a quaint village a few miles from Newquay. Phillip helped his dad build the pretty white-washed building they named Primrose Cottage, and the family moved in early in 1979.

The Schofield's fourth home – Primrose Cottage

A neighbour, Mrs Baines, remembers Phillip being so pleased his mother was going to get a break from running the guest house.

Phillip continued to bombard the BBC with still more letters and, shortly after his 17th birthday his perseverance paid off: he was invited to go to Broadcasting House for an interview for a job as a bookings clerk in the Sport and Outside Broadcasts department in BBC radio.

When his would-be employer expressed concern that someone so young would have to live so far from home, Phillip said he had lots of friends in London. It wasn't true, of course, but having managed to get through the doors of Broadcasting House at last, he was not going to let anything get in the way of a job.

He hoped his white lie put his interviewer's mind at rest, and the day before he was due to leave school, he was overjoyed to learn it had. He got a phone call, telling him the job was his, and would he make plans to move to London.

A bookings clerk may not have been the job that cheerful ten-year-old had dreamed of back in Newquay, but, to the teenage Phillip, the job was fabulous. With an official BBC pass, he had access to all the mysterious places unauthorised people were not allowed to see, and was able to introduce himself to all the disc jockeys he'd seen only on TV or heard on the radio. Asking them all those burning questions stored up over years of ambitious dreaming was arguably the biggest thrill since that memorable summer's day when the Roadshow rolled into town.

Those first six months were, however, difficult for Phillip. He was living in a one-room flat in St John's Wood Terrace, North West London. He never seemed to have much money left out of his £4,500-a-year salary. And, with few friends, he got homesick for Cornwall despite the excitement of his new adventure in London. He would go back to Crantock once a fortnight and enjoy a proper home-cooked meal and a cosy couple of nights at Primrose Cottage. Then it was back to London.

Phillip's job was mainly administrative, which involved organising engineers' rosters and booking out equipment. But the following summer he got the chance to go on outside broadcasts to major events, such as the FA Cup Final at Wembley and the Wimbledon Tennis Championships.

And then, to his joy, he was given some work on Radio One. It was only typing out traffic reports for disc jockeys to read on the air, and it was for only two weeks while someone was on holiday. But, at least, he was in a studio – actually in contact with someone speaking on the radio.

To Phillip, it was a wonderful two-week stint. He revelled in it. He was 19, as cheerful as ever, and getting closer to his dream. He was going places in the BBC.

And then his parents broke the news that they were going to fulfil a dream of their own – they were emigrating to New Zealand.

And it left Phillip with the most agonising decision of his life.

# 3

# Torment in the Sun

The choice was clear-cut, but heartbreakingly tough: Phillip had to choose between throwing away what progress he'd made at the BBC, or being thousands of miles away from his loved ones. It was a no-win situation, but in the end, Phillip chose to join his parents and brother Tim in their adventure down under: they had always been a close-knit family and Phillip knew he would never be happy, however successful he became, with them on the other side of the world.

What convinced him to go was what he had seen first-hand in his two years with the BBC. He had believed that, having broken in, it was only a matter of time before he got the broadcasting job he wanted. But he had found the BBC was like a circle: there were people on the outside, saying: "Super ... terrific ... fabulous ... " but when you came down to it, the real jobs were in the middle, and you needed experience to get there. He could not get that experience in London, but his workmates – particularly a likeable disc jockey, named Peter Powell – said he might be able to make a breakthrough in New Zealand. It was a gamble, but one that Phillip was prepared to take.

He said his goodbyes to the BBC, promising to keep in touch with Peter, and, on September 25, 1981, began the 12,000 mile journey to a new life in the sun.

The family touched down at Auckland's relatively small, but charmingly quaint, airport 28 exhausting hours later, and drove to the city's Pakuranga district, where they rented a house while they looked for something permanent. Phillip's dad had set his heart on living in Howick, a picturesque town overlooking Cockle Bay, and about 40 minutes from the centre of Auckland: he had read about it and even knew the names of some of the roads!

It took the family just three weeks to find their ideal home there – a large, two-bedroomed bungalow in Alexander Street, a short stroll from the beach. The house, Number 15, was perfect, not least because it had loads of space at the side and rear for Brian to extend, and they moved in amid great excitement and expectancy.

Phillip's home in Howick, Auckland

The country was to hold many surprises for the Schofields – and they got their first when they discovered the name of their next door neighbours at Number 13. It was – Schofield.

Harold and Doreen Schofield had moved to Auckland from Sheffield 16 years before and were happily settled in with their two daughters – Catherine, who was 19, and Sally, 12. The families liked each other on sight. Phillip and Catherine, especially, hit it off. They had the same easy-going, light-hearted approach to life and laughed at the same things: Phillip felt so at ease with her. In those first few days they spent a lot of time getting to know each other. It was the start of a deep friendship.

The newly-arrived Schofields adapted quickly to their new life. For Brian, work was no problem: he had arranged a job as a French polisher before leaving England. Tim quickly settled in at the local school and made friends easily. And Phillip launched into another bout of letter-writing – to every radio station in Auckland. The journey had done nothing to change his ambition: he still wanted to be a broadcaster and saw no reason why he couldn't be one. Full of confidence and enthusiasm, he wrote to one producer after another, trying to sell himself – and his limited BBC experience – as best he could.

He did not expect it to be easy: after all, his teachers in Newquay had warned him that broadcasting was a tough business to break into. So, when the first rejections dropped through the letterbox, he was not discouraged: someone, somewhere, he was convinced, would appreciate his potential and give him an interview; it was only a matter of time.

But the weeks passed and the rejections piled up. Sorry, son, most said, you haven't enough experience. Others, more bluntly, sneered: We don't want an English accent on Kiwi radio.

Even for such a resilient and positive thinker as Phillip, the total negative response had a shattering effect. His confidence and self-belief dropped and he began to think that maybe, just maybe, he had blundered in leaving England. For the first time, he pondered on going back. It would be a wrench, a terrible wrench, leaving his family. But, if he stayed, what would he do? He had no idea: he'd only ever considered radio. And even if he managed to get another job, would he be happy in it? Did he really want to stay in a country for the rest of his life doing a job he didn't like? Would it not be best to go back home now, and pick up again with the BBC before it was too late?

The dilemma whirled around in his mind, tormenting him.

The New Zealand Spring turned into a gloriously hot summer, and Brian bought a rubber swimming pool, but Phillip felt guilty laying around the garden. After all day worrying, he would go to bed and lay awake for hours, unable to sleep. He was just 19. And he was at a loss to know what to do for the best.

Next-door neighbour Doreen Schofield witnessed Phillip's anguish first hand. "He tried so hard to get a job – as hard as you can possibly imagine," she says. "He trailed from one radio station to another. He even tried to get work in Wellington, at the end of the North Island, and Christchurch in the South.

"When everyone kept saying No, he would try to put on a brave face and be up about it. Once, he came back from one interview and said he'd been told his voice wasn't deep enough for radio. He tried to make light of it, saying 'I must talk falsetto.' But you could see he was frustrated.

"The longer it went on, the more worried he became. He'd really believed he would get his break here and when it looked like he wouldn't, he started getting very depressed. He'd look at me and say: 'If I can't get in, I don't know what I'm going to do.'

"He'd mope around the house, looking awful. His mum was very worried about him and I remember walking with her, one day, as she talked it out."

Phillip and his family celebrated that Christmas in warm, if unfamiliar, sunshine and he forced himself to look forward to 1982 with optimism. Maybe the New Year would bring a change of luck.

But January came and went. And still no one was willing to take a chance on the young Brit with the burning ambition.

For a long time, the bosses of Television New Zealand had felt they needed a new pop music programme. More to the point, they needed a producer who knew what the country's kids wanted to see. The man they turned to was Peter Grattan, noted for his enthusiasm and love of music. At the time, Peter was producing sports programmes, but the employers of the Government-owned station felt he had the qualities for the pop job. After all, he had a band of his own: P.G. and the Hot Tips.

Peter was thrilled at the prospect of putting together a pop programme of his own, but shocked at the deadline for getting it on the screen. He had just six weeks, his employers told him, to create the format, think of ideas, and find the people to put the whole thing into practice. With the pressure on, however, ideas began to flow. What young Kiwi pop fans wanted were interviews with famous stars, video and film reviews and a fashion spot. Peter set these in motion, and other ideas quickly followed.

So did a name for the show. Peter wanted something catchy and he came up with a word he remembered from his childhood: Shazam! It was what the American comic hero Captain Marvel shouted to transform himself from a crippled newspaper boy into a Superman-like crimefighter – and Peter felt it was perfect.

Within days, he had everything for his show, except a person to present it. He came up with a novel idea for this, too: he would have not just one presenter, but two. And they would not be familiar "star" faces the kids knew – they would be unknowns. A young man and a young woman.

Having the idea was one thing; finding two unknowns with the right qualities among Auckland's sports-crazy kids was another. With time against him, Peter took a short cut: he arranged for a story to appear in the city's biggest daily newspaper, revealing details of the new programme, and inviting youngsters to audition.

The story appeared on Page 13 of the Auckland Star on Monday, February 15. It was only ten paragraphs and buried amid the TV listings, but Peter prayed it would do the trick.

Certainly the paper had played fair with him. The headline ran: POP SHOW WANTS FRONTPERSONS and the third paragraph said that Peter Grattan wanted to find "two, not one, young or thereabouts, presenters for the show". To Peter's delight, the point was made even more forcibly in the last two paragraphs:

*Meantime, there is a terrific opportunity for a host and hostess. If you are in your 20s, say, and live in Auckland, it could be the musical door by which you break into showbiz.*

*You will need to know your music, be involved in the current pop scene ... and have that indefinable thing, a TV presence.*

Peter read the story and smiled: it was perfect. Surely, there must be thousands of young people who would grab the chance of a crack at stardom; thousands who would read those words and think excitedly: "That's me."

Early that Monday evening, Harold Schofield, was reading the Star in his lounge. Wanting to know what was on television, he turned to the programme listings. He wasn't the least interested in what was new on the pop scene, but, for some reason he still cannot explain, he was drawn to the story about Shazam!

## Pop show wants frontpersons

15-2-82

The new pop show to replace *Drop of Culture*, if you will excuse the correct spelling, is *Shazam!*

It may bring back fond memories to Captain Marvel fans — he used to say it before turning into a super crime-fighter ... Or was it Superman?

Anyway, *Shazam!* is the name producer Peter Grattan has chosen for the new-look pop slot and he wants to find two, not one, young or thereabouts presenters for the show.

One of them will be a woman.

"We believe a host and a hostess will be a good idea," he says. "Anyone interested just has to apply."

That means, of course, that Dropa Kulcha frontman Terry Herbert has been lost in the musical shuffle that should see a new look, even if it turns out to be a slightly dated '60s look, to the new programme.

Peter Grattan, who has his own group, says fans can request videos ... there will be chats about fashion ...

backgrounders on big names in rock .. even film reviews.

The series begins on April 7 and the new look comes about because Andy Shaw, who was once the *Dropa Kulcha* kid, is now working on the TV version of Mercury's *Kiwi Concert Party* show and Bryan Easte will take over production of *Chic Chat*.

There will even be a revamping of the Duane Eddy song *Shazam* as the signature tune for the show, if you'll forgive such an old-fashioned word. The revamping will be new wave style, of course.

Meantime, there is a terrific opportunity for a host and hostess. If you are in your 20s, say, and live in Auckland it could be the musical door by which you break into show biz.

You will need to know your music, be involved in the current pop scene ... and have that indefinable thing, a TV presence.

The newspaper story that sparked Phillip's TV career in New Zealand

When he read that third paragraph, an idea began to form in his mind. By the time he'd got to the end of the story, he was positively excited and called out to his wife, Doreen: "Have a look at this, love. It's right up our Phillip's street."

Doreen agreed.

More excited than ever, the friendly, forthright Yorkshireman went round to Number 15. He found Phillip alone, looking glum as usual. Handing him the paper, folded at Page 13, Harold said, bluntly: "That's just the job for you, son. You'll get that dead easy."

Intrigued, Phillip took the paper and read the story. But then he shook his head. "Thanks, Harold," he said. "It sounds good. But it's not right for me. I want to do radio."

Today, Harold says: "I shouldn't have been surprised by his reaction. Ever since he arrived, radio was all Phillip would talk about. But I felt he had so much personality he'd be wasted on radio because no one would be able to see him. I tried to tell him he'd be great on TV and this was his big chance, but Phillip wasn't convinced. I didn't go on about it, though, because it was his life and he knew what he wanted to do."

After talking it over with his mum, however, Phillip changed his mind. With no prospect of any other job on the horizon, he felt he had nothing to lose by trying for an audition. Now well versed in the art of job applications, he wrote to Peter Grattan and quickly got TVNZ's reply, telling him that auditions were being held on the first Friday in March at studios in Shortland Street, in Auckland's city centre.

Phillip was pleased, but not all that hopeful; his morale was low and he felt he'd be just one of many applicants. The odds, he told his family and the friendly couple next door, were against him.

But Harold, said: "If they don't pick you lad, they're a bit short on top. It'll be them who've missed out."

And he meant it.

Over the next few days, Phillip's mum and dad boosted him up, too, and he began to get more and more excited – and confident.

Catherine Schofield's boyfriend, Bruce Copeland, remembers seeing Phillip on the Thursday night before the Friday audition and thinking how relaxed he was.

"He was ultra-confident and underplaying the whole thing," says Bruce. "You'd say, 'Go for it, Phillip, good luck' – yet have the feeling he didn't need it. It was as if he felt there was nothing he couldn't do."

New Zealand is a casual country, but Phillip put on his smartest clothes for the audition the following night. He knew he had the ability to do what was required, but he wanted to look good, too.

Peter Grattan was disappointed with the response to the newspaper story. He didn't get hundreds of applications; he got just 35. To make matters worse, he was on such a low budget for Shazam! that he had only one hour's studio time, over two evenings, to test his would-be TV stars.

The first set of hopefuls were given a script and told they had one minute in front of the camera to tell imaginary viewers about the new pop programme. Then, they would link a pop video with a voice-over and close the show.

It sounded simple enough and Peter started rolling the cameras, hoping for the best. But after seeing 14 "presenters", however, he was a worried man. The candidates were nice enough people and all were trying their hardest, but none had the sparkle he was searching for. None stood a chance of landing the job.

And then the 15th applicant, a tall, skinny lad with a cheeky look, came into the studio and sat in front of the camera.

And the second Peter heard him speak he had a feeling that at least half his problems were over.

"Hello," the boy said into the camera, beaming brightly. "My name is Phillip Schofield. And I'm your host for Shazam! We're going to be here every week with the latest from the pop charts ..."

The words came out in a smooth, confident, well-spoken tone. But it was not only what he heard that impressed Peter Grattan – it was what he saw.

Phillip was at ease in front of the camera. And the camera simply loved him. He was a natural.

Peter will never forget that evening. "The more we saw of Phillip on screen, the more excited the control room got," he says. "About halfway through Phillip's minute, there was this big sort of 'wow' feeling – that he was the guy we'd all been looking for. The weeks were ticking away and everyone was worried we weren't going to find anyone suitable, and it was a great relief to see Phillip so good. He was by far the best of everyone I'd seen and I couldn't have hoped for anyone better. To be honest, my mind was made up even before he'd finished his audition.

"You know when you've found someone special. Some kids are just announcers who merely say the words, but others come out at you from the screen. Phillip was one of those. He spoke to the viewer, not the camera, in a very natural manner.

"He didn't look like the average kid. He was apprehensive, like the others, because he knew this was his big chance. But he had a certain control over his nerves.

"When he had finished, none of us let on how much he'd impressed us. I just said, 'Thank you – we'll let you know.'

"But as soon as he had gone I told the remaining candidates they were not needed. With time so short, I'd decided to forget the idea of a female presenter and to go solely with Phillip. I cancelled the auditions planned for the following evening.

"The next week I asked Phillip to come to my office, but I still didn't tell him immediately he had the job. With so little money to play with, I was worried he would ask for too much if he knew I wanted him that badly. So we just had a chat and kicked around ideas. He had loads of his own that impressed me.

"After about an hour, I told him he had the job and he would be paid £100 a week. He was delighted – completely blown away."

Phillip walked out of Peter's office into Shortland Street in a daze. He was slightly concerned that he'd added a couple of years to his age and exaggerated his BBC experience, but the worries had gone by the time he reached Alexander Street. He had got the job. And he knew he'd be good at it. That was all that mattered. After six months of agonising rejection, of moping about the house, depressed at getting nowhere, he had been given a chance. It wasn't radio, but it was a job. And at £100 a week.

Doreen could not wait to hear what had happened. "How did it go?" she said excitedly. "How did you get on?"

Phillip looked at her, not giving anything away for a second. Then he said, casually: "I'm going to be on the television."

And he beamed.

# 4

# The Milky Bar Kids

The following Monday, March 8, Phillip walked into the New Zealand Television offices and took the lift to the third floor where he was to work. If he was disappointed at his small, partitioned office, he didn't show it. After the usual introductions, he sat behind his desk and got to work; there was lots to do. The first programme was being recorded in just two weeks – desperately little time for him to get in tune with the New Zealand music scene and find out about new releases and which recording stars were available for interview.

Phillip quickly found TV had one huge advantage over radio. Since he would be seen as well as heard, he was given a small clothing allowance to sharpen up his image. He was always smart, if casual, but Shazam! was a trend-setting young people's show, and Peter wanted him in the very latest, and expensive, "designer" gear. So, he recommended a fashionable clothes store and told Phillip to buy himself some T-shirts, trousers and jeans. For a young man who had spent the previous six months wondering what to do with himself, it was an unexpected and exhilarating experience, and Phillip was so excited, he couldn't wait to show off what he had bought.

"He was really happy," Doreen recalls. "It was a case of, 'Look what I've got.' I was so, so pleased for him."

Phillip's first interview was with Cliff Richard, along with dozens of other radio, TV and newspaper journalists. The record company had briefed them that Cliff would be doing a question and answer conference and there would be no opportunity for one-to-one personal interviews. The older, more experienced, reporters were happy with this and disappeared quickly afterwards, but Phillip was not satisfied. He badly wanted a personal interview with Cliff for his first show and felt it was worth a try asking him. He waited his moment, then went up to Cliff and, very politely, asked if he would mind answering just two more questions for the camera. Whether it was Phillip's cheek that did it, is not clear, but something about the fresh-faced youngster's approach appealed to the legendary British singer – because he didn't stop talking for 17 minutes. Phillip could not believe his luck.

The big day was Monday, March 22 – the day when Shazam! was to be recorded, for its first screening on April 7. A lot of effort had gone into getting the show off the ground in such a short time and everyone was keyed up. Phillip, however, was more than that – he was downright nervous. And the production crew spotted it.

Jim Biggam, the floor manager, says: "We tried to ease him into the recording by taking our time and re-taking shots, so that he got the hang of things. But his nerves made his face stiffen in front of the camera. I'd worked with famous actresses, such as Glenda Jackson, and I told him to do what they do, which is pretend the camera is a person. I moved as close as I could to it, so that he could easily have been speaking to me. It seemed to help. And we all discovered very soon afterwards that Phillip had a natural gift for the camera.

"Something that struck me very early on was his brilliant memory. We'd change his script and he'd read it through once, then say: 'Okay, right, let's do it.' And he'd say it straight off, no problem." Shazam! went out on TVNZ's Channel One at 5.30 p.m. on Wednesday, April 7, aimed at children between 12 and 17. Video footage of soul singer George Benson at his Auckland concert opened the show with: "Hi, I'm George Benson and this is Shazam!" Some cartoons followed, then Phillip was on screen, telling viewers what to expect from the 30-minute show.

Everyone connected with the programme was pleased. Considering it had been put together quickly, on a low budget, it had gone remarkably smoothly and well. And it would get better.

Phillip, it seemed that night, had been a success. Ross Goodwin, who did the live voice-over links between programmes, remembers thinking: Wow, he looks great. The camera loves him. And the kids will, too.

Today, Ross says: "Phillip's hair-cut wasn't exactly hip, but he was fresh and had hot looks. He was suitably nervous, but had a presence and a smile which made everyone feel good about watching him. His English accent didn't seem to scare the hell out of the TV bosses – he was too good in many other ways."

The Auckland Herald's TV critic, Richard Moore, liked Phillip's debut, too. He felt he spoke a little too quickly at times, and he didn't care for the cheeky wink at the end of the programme. But he praised Phillip's coolness and maturity.

If the Shazam! team had high ideas that they had hit the jackpot first time out, they were brought down to earth with an almighty bump by another critic.

The Auckland Star's Kirsten Warner hated the show. And she didn't like Phillip, particularly his accent.

"Isn't there a Kiwi kid out there who could front Shazam!?" was her opening snipe. And she went on to slate the show.

Warner's criticism was a body blow to the programme and Phillip in particular; and had it not been for Peter Grattan, the newest face on New Zealand television might possibly have vanished as quickly as it had appeared. First, Peter wrote a long, well-constructed letter to the Star in Phillip's defence, pointing out that he'd been by far the most talented of those he had auditioned; and that Kirsten Warner's criticism was the only unfavourable words he'd heard or read. Then, Peter sent copies of the letter to all the key bosses in the Children's Programme Department. He had faith in the show. He had faith in Phillip. And he wanted everyone to know it.

There was never any question of scrapping the programme; the station was committed to recording 13 shows – one a week – up to June 28. But what would happen after that was anyone's guess.

Certainly fellow TV workers did not take it seriously in the beginning. And they were indifferent to Phillip, too. Most felt he was a nice enough kid in a pretty ordinary show.

Andrew Shaw, a popular presenter, whose show, Dropa Kulcha, was axed to make way for Shazam! says: "Phillip's first appearances weren't hesitant ones you'd expect from someone just starting out; he was quite polished. But TV in New Zealand wasn't particulary sophisticated then, and, to be honest, nobody really noticed Shazam!, or cared. It was put together in the children's department on a shoestring budget and Phillip would have been on peaknuckle money. Everyone I spoke to felt the show would disappear after the first series."

They were all wrong. The kids loved Shazam! And after a 10-week winter break, it came back with another 13 weekly shows. More and more viewers were switching on every week and Phillip's popularity began to grow. Those who had written off the efforts of the hard-working third-floor team were forced to take the show, and its presenter, seriously.

Even Andrew admits: "It was impossible not to take notice of Phillip. He was becoming a star. He had talent, of course, but he had that all-important X-factor, too – the quality that makes some people stand out and be noticed. Those without the X-factor can be in a room with a lot of people all night and never be noticed. Phillip wasn't like that. He most definitely had the X-factor – on camera and off it. And he had the same ageless appeal as Cliff Richard – the sort of boy any mother wouldn't mind their daughter bringing home. He was safe and clean and nice and fresh. As more kids watched, the more adults seemed to take notice as well."

Not surprisingly, Phillip's fan mail increased and he took a pride in replying to every one personally. He was thrilled, of course, but more important to him was his performance on screen and he bought a video recorder to see where he was going wrong.

Production assistant Louise Jones says: "Phillip taped every show and if he saw something he didn't like, he made sure he changed it for the next one. Every now and again, he would even watch shows he'd done months before, to see how much he had improved. He took great care and pride in his work."

When you think how rare VCRs were in the early eighties, it is easy to appreciate just how dedicated he was.

To his mum and dad and the neighbouring Schofields, Phillip was the same as he'd always been. But to the thousands of young Shazam! fans, he was now a Face – someone to stare at, to point to, and to have sign autographs. Phillip would look at the reflection in a shop window on his way to work and see young girls pointing at him behind his back. And he'd go home and tell Doreen Schofield: "I think they knew who I was."

People would shout at him as he walked by. When he left the studio at lunchtime and queued for a hamburger, he'd notice people staring at him. And then, as his fame grew, fans wanted him to sign his name.

Phillip loved the attention, but he never got big-headed. If anything, it would amuse him and he'd take the mickey out of himself.

Doreen remembers laughing one day when he came home and said: "A funny thing happened today – someone asked for my autograph. Why do people want MY autograph?"

"You stupid idiot," Doreen said. "Why do you think? You're a TV star."

"Oh, fancy that," Phillip replied, casually.

He was only 20. He took his job seriously. He did not see himself as famous.

And if he did begin to get carried away, there was always his mother there to keep his feet on the ground. "Don't let all this success go to your head, young man," she would say. "You're no different from anyone else. And you're still my lad."

There was little chance of Phillip changing: his background was too secure, and he had worked too hard, tasted rejection too much, to believe his own publicity.

That's why he made fun of himself at home after the TV company printed postcards of his photograph for him to sign for his adoring female fans.

Phillip was thrilled by the cards. Which 20-year-old wouldn't be? But he saw the funny side, too, and he would sign them for the Schofields and their daughters, Catherine and Sally, laughing: "Here we are – the star signing autographs."

One of Phillip's publicity postcards

The bond between Phillip and Catherine had grown stronger. She was such good fun and Phillip loved spending time with her. They would even walk along Alexander Street to Litten Road together every morning to catch the 7.30 a.m. single-decker bus into Auckland. Then they would share a Milky Bar, along Queen Street, before going to their respective offices.

Like her mum, Catherine enjoyed living next door to a personality, especially since she had known him in the beginning when he was unknown, and she made sure she was home from work in time to watch Shazam! on Wednesday evenings. Catherine and her younger sister, Sally, would call out to their mum: "Hurry up – he's just about to speak." And Doreen would stop what she was doing in the kitchen and rush in to watch the show with them.

"We'd never miss Phillip, even though I'd curse him for having his show just when I'd be making dinner," Doreen jokes.

Doreen enjoyed the reflective glory in the nicest possible way. With the same surname, people naturally assumed she was Phillip's mother and she lost count of the times she had to put them right. It happened most when she went shopping in Howick and signed cheques. Cashiers would look at the name and, nine times out of ten, say: "Are you Phillip Schofield's mum?"

Ready for it, Doreen would shake her head, tolerantly, and say: "No, love, I'm his next-door neighbour."

That would floor them. They wouldn't know if she was kidding.

Today, Doreen remembers those early days of Phillip's fame with great affection, particularly when he used to pop round the day before his programme to show her what he'd be wearing.

"He was so genuine and natural," she says. "He was interested in what I thought. I tried to be honest and told him if he looked smart or whatever. He was such a nice lad. But it wasn't just us who got on well with him – everyone in the street liked him."

Towards the end of the second Shazam! series, in November 1982, Phillip's serious approach to work was disrupted by a wave of euphoria that swept through the office: he had been nominated for an award at the annual New Zealand Music Awards.

It was a big night, not only for Phillip, but for Peter Grattan and the whole team. And, of course, it was a posh affair – with all the men in tuxedos and the ladies in evening gowns or party dresses.

Thrilled at the prospect of winning a national award after such a short time in the country, Phillip went shopping – with company money again – to hire a dinner suit, frilled shirt and bow tie. He was so excited. He'd never dressed up like it in his life.

A couple of days before the ceremony, he put on the suit to show his mum and dad how he looked. Then he popped next door to see what the Schofields thought. They'd only ever seen him in casual clothes and were amazed.

"He looked really super," Doreen recalls. "But suddenly we noticed that something wasn't quite right. It was his shoes. Instead of a nice shiny black leather pair, he was wearing a pair of soft, casual boots, and they let the whole outfit down.

"'You can't walk in wearing them, Phillip,' we all said."

Phillip agreed; he'd thought that himself. But he spent all his time in casual gear and the boots were the most appropriate footwear he'd been able to find.

Catherine's boyfriend, Bruce, came to the rescue. He was an accountant and had just the pair Phillip needed. He dashed home to get them, while everyone kept their fingers crossed they fitted.

Bruce came back with a pair of shiny black ankle boots. All eyes on him, Phillip tried them on. They fitted perfectly, and set off his whole look wonderfully. Everyone cheered: "Hooray," and Phillip gave a catwalk-style twirl, beaming broadly. He looked stunning.

Predictably, Phillip saw the funny side, and started making an acceptance speech, as though he had won his award.

"He hammed it up and had us all in fits," Bruce remembers. "He didn't say all the usual things, like, 'I must thank my producers, and my mum for having me,' and all that sort of thing. Instead, he said: "I must thank Bruce Copeland for lending me the shoes, such and such shop for lending me the suit etcetera, etcetera ... "

Sadly, Phillip didn't get an award. But he had a fabulous night. Despite his growing fame, he was, in many ways, still an innocent, feeling excitement at everything that was opening up for him.

Shazam! was a national success, but no one would have guessed it if they had seen the cramped office Phillip and Co. moved into, just around the corner, in Queen Street. It was in the middle of a huge building, called Centre Court, and the production team didn't have one window between them!

It was absurd. They were making one of the brightest, most colourful shows on television, and they were doing it in the dullest, most unglamorous surroundings imaginable. The irony was not lost on Phillip and his colleagues and they would make fun of it.

Gray Taylor, a director on the show, says; "We developed a gallows humour among ourselves. We had to. The office was so grim we'd have gone crazy if we hadn't made fun of it.

"We had no idea what it was like in the outside world – not even what the weather was like. Around lunchtime, I'd say: 'I wonder if the weather is nice enough to go out?' – and Phillip would immediately jump on his desk to look across adjoining offices to a window at the far end of the building to give me a weather report.

"We were an incredibly small-scale operation, on a shoestring budget, and had to make do with the most antiquated equipment. We'd all throw mock tantrums until, eventually, the awfulness of it all became a running joke."

The success of Shazam! depended on Phillip's personality and the pressure on him was intense. There was always a limited time for recording, so he had to try to get things right first time, to save running through large chunks of the show again. To his credit, he and the whole operation worked exceptionally well, as Gray Taylor is quick to recognise.

"With Phillip on top of his job, it was effortless for me as director," he says. "When there was a break, he'd continue chatting to the crew as normal. There was very little change, or acting, for him once he was on camera. His personality was only slightly amplified on screen."

What made Phillip so popular among his colleagues, it seems, was his modesty and naturalness. Many had seen nice people turn into nasty prima donnas with TV exposure, but Phillip never once played the "star".

Nor did he run around the office, yelling and screaming, to let everyone know he was under pressure or working hard. He just put his head down and got on with his work quietly.

Fritha Goodman, a producer's assistant, who worked just along the corridor, says: "Never once did I hear him complain about the down side of his job – like writing schedules for production meetings or scripts. Nor did he moan about the long hours he sometimes had to work. He never shirked his responsibility. He was always there, always enthusiastic.

"He was desperately keen and seemed to put 110 per cent into his work. He would have to chase record companies for permission to record at a concert or do a "special", and, listening to him, you could almost feel his determination. When he got his way, you could sense his satisfaction and relief.

"He and Peter had desks opposite each other and they were like little boys, bouncing ideas around and feeding off each other. Once they'd hit on something, one or the other would shout: 'Great. Let's do it.' You could see the excitement on Phillip's face.

"The mood in the office was nearly always good, but it was great when the ratings came in. You knew when they'd arrived because there was so much more noise – and, if Shazam's ratings had risen, Phillip and Peter would go beserk. Not that there was any extra money in it for Phillip. The popularity of the programme had nothing to do with how much one was paid.

"It was a Government company and Phillip would get an annual rise, based on the grade system, not ratings success. No one would come round to his office to acknowledge his achievements. One got a visit only when something was wrong."

The fact that Shazam! – and Phillip – was not doing anything wrong was reflected in a top-level decision early in 1983. The big wigs of TVNZ told Grattan he would have 45 shows that year.

The show – moved to the same time on Tuesdays – introduced a Video Vault spot, in which Phillip moved around in a mock cellar, with cobwebs and skeletons, and showed footage from the sixties, featuring the Beatles, Rolling Stones, Animals and other top bands. Phillip showed great flair for ad-libbing: he would make witty remarks if he bumped into a skeleton; and Gray Taylor remembers him grabbing one and going into an impromptu waltz.

Phillip had been in the business just 12 months, but his performance now had all the maturity of a veteran, and it was not surprising, that Spring, that his image changed rather dramatically.

He had come into TVNZ a raw kid with it all to prove. Now, as he approached his 21st birthday in April, he had become an elegant young man, with the country, if not the world, at his feet.

And he felt he ought to change his hairstyle to help the part.

# 5

# Close-Up On Romance

The new style, made even more fashionable with hair gel, helped make Phillip look more sophisticated, less cute. And, not surprisingly, the first ones to notice were the girls.

Louise Jones was most impressed. "Suddenly he was a yummy, good-looking man about town – but without bags of ego," she says. "He was so nice and friendly that girls around the office went out of their way to see that he was all right. He was very slim, so one of us sorted out sweatshirts, padded at the shoulders, with a criss-cross design, to fill him out a little. That whooshed up his image still more.

"No matter how successful he got, however, he always took his turn making the tea. He never got dictatorial, never expected to be waited on. He was generous, too. When we went to the cinema, he was the perfect gentleman and insisted on paying for me. He was always very giving like that.

"Over coffee once, he let me into a secret. 'You know what I really want to do one day, Louise,' he said. 'I want to act. I would love to do something really big.'

"He said he'd done a little bit of acting at school and was quite serious about doing it for real. He'd entertained us with stories and funny accents and looked great on screen, so I said I'd look out for a part for him. I did actually put him up for a TV drama, but, sadly nothing came of it."

By this time Phillip had bought himself a car – a green Hillman Hunter. But it was a bad buy and forever breaking down. Typically,

Phillip saw the funny side and had his colleagues laughing with the trials and tribulations the car gave him.

He'd kid them that he had to reverse down roads because he couldn't get the car to go forward. And when he eventually sold it, he'd say his life wasn't nearly so interesting because all the new car would do was run properly!

Outside work, too, life was one long round of fun for Phillip. There was no romance in his life, but over the months he and Catherine had got even closer, in a brother and sister sort of way.

"They were great mates – certainly best friends," says Bruce Copeland. "They seemed to have so much fun together and it was always positive fun, never at someone else's expense.

"She was a really happy girl and he was always full of beans – they were a good match, always seeing the funny side of things and getting up to crazy antics.

"Once, I went to Phillip's house and found he and Catherine and Sally dressed up in some old clothes, acting some play they'd made up. The television was on, but no one was watching. They were good at making their own fun and horsing around. They seemed able to laugh at anything.

"Catherine was into sport and would always be trying to coax Phillip into going for a run. But he was very non-athletic and, no matter how hard she tried, she couldn't make him budge from the garden.

"She was good at squash and tried to teach him. But Phillip was so unco-ordinated, he missed the ball every time he tried to serve. Then, we organised games of cricket in the back garden, but I'm afraid Phillip had trouble hitting that ball as well. We all fell about laughing."

The joke may have been on Phillip then, but, only a few months before, he'd had Catherine and her family laughing with him.

It was Catherine's 21st birthday on February 16, and Phillip played a starring role to make the barbecue evening an extra special occasion for her. First, he rigged up a microphone and music system in the garden. Then, he took the mike and led the 40 guests singing Happy Birthday.

Immediately after the song, Phillip vanished, then reappeared behind a bush a few minutes later – and did a brilliant impression of David Bellamy.

Catherine's mother Doreen found it hilarious. She says: "Some people might be able to do the voice, but wouldn't know which words to say. Phillip did. He was probably mumbling rubbish, but it somehow sounded right – and just like David Bellamy. I was crying with laughter. I'll never forget his face as he delved into the bush and examined the leaves. He was a really talented mimic."

If Phillip was looking for romance at that time, he didn't show it. There were plenty of girls around and he got on well with them, and vice versa. But, as with Catherine, that was as far as it went. He was in love with his work; most, if not all, his time was spent thinking about that.

But then a pretty blonde girl came to the studios to train as a floor manager. Her name was Marika Tautz. She was 19 and half-Russian.

And Phillip couldn't take his eyes off her.

What he didn't know was that Marika couldn't take her eyes off him! After work she would go home, to Milford, on the North Shore, and tell her mother, Miriam, all about "this young, really good-looking guy in the office."

"Jim Biggam, the floor manager, introduced us," Marika remembers today. "I'd broken up with someone else and I guess Jim mentioned to Phil that I was unattached.

"We were recording one day, and, during a break, he came up and started chatting. I found him a really genuine and down-to-earth guy."

Secretly, Marika hoped Phillip would ask her out, and a few weeks later he did. He took her to lunch at a restaurant in the Parnell district of Auckland – the equivalent of Chelsea – and they hit it off. Marika was the envy of her friends: she had gone out with a Star, *the* wonderful Phillip Schofield. And they demanded to know as much about him as Marika could tell; every detail.

To satisfy their curiosity, Marika decided to hold a small cocktail party so that her friends could meet him for themselves. She persuaded her parents to go to the cinema for the evening, and threw herself into putting on a super evening, with strange-sounding, exotic cocktails, served in the proper glasses.

Miriam remembers the evening well. "Marika was clearly quite thrilled to have Phillip and her friends around," she says. "It was a big thing for her and it was really the beginning of their relationship. After that, they were together all the time.

"My husband and I didn't get to know him well at all that evening. When we came home from the pictures, Marika introduced us, but we just said, Hello. I did think he was a nice-looking, courteous, young man, though, and I was happy later when we began to see a lot of him.

Phillip and Marika share a joke together

"He and Marika were delightful together and had a lovely relationship. They were like a couple of young puppies, running around the house and chasing each other up and down the stairs, and, in hot weather, turning the hose on each other in the garden. They had so much fun.

"Phillip was thoroughly nice and entertaining to have around. His eyes sparkled with his personality and he talked flat out, gesticulating all the time. When he came round, we all stopped what we were doing and sat around listening to him and laughing at his stories. He was a fun-loving boy – like a breath of fresh air.

"If I was cooking in the kitchen, he'd look in the pot, give me a grin and say: 'Ooooh, that smells nice. Can I stay for tea?'

"Afterwards, he'd help clear the table and do the washing up with Marika. We'd hear them giggling and screaming in the kitchen. But they got the job done eventually.

"Phillip talked about his fame, but said he'd never get carried away by it. I believed him, then, and still do.

"He was excited about the progress he was making, though. Once, he asked, 'Did you see my write-up in The Listener?' When I said I hadn't, he rushed to his car to get it. He wasn't being big-headed, just full of enthusiasm.

"I loved talking to him. He was so sincere and would look straight into your eyes as he told you what he was doing and how he felt."

At the start of the New Zealand winter – the British summer – Phillip was working hard, and feeling great.

And then, one day in June, Doreen and Harold Schofield told him some awful news that ripped him apart and broke his heart.

Catherine, their lovely, young, fun-loving daughter, had a rare cancer. She had little hope; little time.

Phillip's close friend, Catherine, on her 21st birthday, six months before she died

# 6

# Tears for a Friend

Phillip could not believe it. No one could. One minute Catherine was running around, full of fun, full of life; the next, she was dying. Both Schofield families reeled, shocked and devastated.

Phillip felt it deeply: he and Catherine had been so close; he liked her so much. He went next door to comfort Doreen and she ended up comforting him.

"He was so cut up," Doreen recalls, sadly. "He said he couldn't believe it, couldn't get over it. I did my best to comfort him and we cried together."

Poor Catherine faded tragically quickly and, in the third week of August, was taken into hospital. Phillip went to see her there with Marika and did his best to cheer her up. But he found it hard to fight back his tears, and when it got near the end, he was too upset to go.

He told Doreen: "I can't face it. I know I'll just break down."

Catherine died on Monday, August 29, and Phillip wrote a poignant letter to Doreen and Harold telling them that their daughter had been a "beautiful lady".

Doreen says today: "The letter was so unexpected. You don't think young boys will do things like that. But underneath that laughing, joking veneer, Phillip was a deeply caring, sensitive boy, and he was terribly broken up that Catherine had been taken in such a tragic way. They'd known each other for only a short time, but they had been terrific friends."

# 7

# Live, Dad, Live!

One day, Phillip may want to talk publicly about Catherine and the effect her sudden death had on him, and his attitude to life. Certainly it cut deeply into him, and he took a long time coming to terms with it, while continuing to work flat out in a high-pressure job. And it is clear that, in the weeks after the tragedy, Marika saw a quieter, more reflective side to him that had not been evident in their carefree relationship. Since their meeting, he had bubbled incessantly, dazzling her with his infectious, effervescent personality, insatiable appetite for work and general joie de vivre; but now, as the New Zealand winter drew on, there were times when he became withdrawn, sombre almost, and would insist on being alone.

While working late sometimes, he would suddenly leave the office and go up on the roof and just sit there, gazing into the night and up at the stars.

Marika would ask him where he was going, but he'd say he wanted to be by himself. "He was quite happy alone," she says. "He was a boy who was quite content with his own company."

Workwise, he was hot. The kids loved him; so did their mums. He was in great demand, and offers to present or appear on other shows rolled in. He became a regular panellist on a programme called Starquest. He presented another children's show, Freetime, throughout the school holidays. And then, on September 9, he was chosen to host the first live radio/TV simulcast for the 1983 Battle of the Bands contest at Auckland's YMCA stadium.

With Shazam! still going out every week, Phillip was so busy he had to postpone a much-needed skiing holiday with Marika at Mount Hutt in the South Island. They finally made it later that year, but no sooner had Phillip come back than another emotional trauma rocked his life.

It involved his dad.

Brian Schofield had always been proud of his fitness. In his younger days, he played soccer at good club standard. In his forties, he kept in trim with long walks along the Cornish beaches. And, of course, there was his DIY. It was physically demanding, but Brian loved it. He was one of those active men who thrived on being busy.

Now, enjoying the outdoor life that New Zealand's climate provided, Brian celebrated his 48th birthday in September, feeling great. True, his father had died of a heart attack at the same age – and his brother even earlier, at 42. But Brian saw no reason to worry about his own health. He looked young. And he felt it. He rarely had an ache in his body, even after his tiring DIY. He felt on top of the world.

One night, early in November, Phillip drove to Marika's home. He wanted to go to the cinema, but, it seems, she was in a bad mood and wanted to stay in. Disappointed, Phillip stayed for only a few minutes, then got in his car and drove home.

That 40-minute drive was to be the most crucial journey of his life. It was as if fate had decided he should be with his family, not Marika, that night.

Earlier that evening, Phillip's dad had gone to an art class in Howick. When he came out, he found he couldn't get into his car because he had mistakenly locked the keys inside. It was a nuisance, because Alexander Street was a few miles away, but Brian was not unduly bothered. It was a spring evening and a leisurely stroll in the warm coastal air would be good for him, he thought.

Brian set off, feeling as fit as usual. But by the time he reached his neighbourhood and climbed Granger Road – the hill that leads to Alexander Street – he was quite exhausted. When he got home, Phillip and the rest of the family were there. Brian slumped breathlessly into an armchair.

Suddenly he complained of feeling dizzy. Pat was horrified to see the colour draining from his face. Worried, she called out to Phillip to ring an ambulance.

In the next few seconds, Brian collapsed in his chair, dying from a massive heart attack.

Immediately, Pat and Tim started massaging Brian's heart, trying to revive him. Pat had worked with old people and seen them collapse, but she did not know precisely what to do for Brian. Seconds later, Phillip came off the phone. He stared at his dad, lying on the floor, ashen-faced and still, and his mum doing her best for him.

"Mum," he cried. "You're not doing it right."

Then he knelt beside him and started thumping his dad's chest and trying the kiss of life, willing him to breathe again.

But his mother was convinced Brian had gone. She grabbed Phillip and Tim and sobbed: "He's dead. He's dead."

Suddenly, she remembered that Doreen next door was a Brownie leader and had done a First Aid course a few weeks before. Pat knew that a heart attack victim could survive for just four minutes. After that, it was too late.

In a wild panic, she ran round to the back of Doreen's house, screaming hysterically: "Brian's dead … Brian's dead."

Doreen will never forget Pat's terror. "Her scream sent a chill through me," she says. "She was yelling at the top of her voice. Harold and I rushed out of our house. It had been little more than two months since Catherine had died and I remember thinking. 'Please God, don't let me see another person die.'

"We went into Pat's lounge and saw Phillip leaning on his dad's chest, doing heart massage. Brian wasn't breathing. His face was marble white and his eyes closed. I knew he was dead immediately.

And Phillip thought so, too. There was terror in his eyes and we could see he thought his dad had had it.

"But he wasn't panicking. He was thumping Brian's chest and massaging him, then thumping him again, all the time shouting: 'You're not going to die, dad. You're not going to die. You're not going yet.'

"Phillip was unaware of us. His eyes were fixed on his dad and he was going mad and shaking; and he kept shouting, over and over again: 'Live, dad. LIVE! You've got to LIVE!'

"I don't think I'll ever see anything like it in my life again. Phillip was determined that if his will could bring his father back, he would find it. And he did. He willed his dad back to life. He was mad with anger that he was going to lose his dad and the anger gave him the strength to keep going.

"I never thought once of taking over. I could see Phillip was hitting the right spot and knew what he was doing. He had his left hand on his dad's chest and was thumping it with his right.

"'Keep going, Phillip,' I kept telling him. 'You're saving your dad's life.'"

Suddenly a gurgling sound came from Brian's throat and his chest heaved; he was trying to breathe. Noticing that his head was leaning back in the wrong postion, Doreen bent down and turned it on its side: all the fluid blocking Brian's throat flowed out on to the carpet, and he started to breathe.

"Again, dad," Phillip pleaded. "Again. Do it *again.*"

Brian started to take deeper breaths. Phillip seemed to have won his fight for life. But, just as the ambulancemen knocked on the door, he faded and Phillip had to bring him round again. The ambulancemen ran in.

"Good lad," one of them said to Phillip. "Keep doing what you're doing." And then, seconds later, they brought in a portable machine to keep Brian's heart going on the way to the hospital. But he regained consciousness before they could get him in the ambulance and he tried to refuse to go, claiming he had recovered and was okay.

He was taken to hospital, of course, and kept in for a full examination. Phillip went, too, for a test of his own: his left hand was swollen and it was feared he'd broken a bone, thumping it so hard. An X-ray showed nothing was broken, but a blood vessel had burst.

For Phillip, it was a tiny, insignificant, price for saving his dad's life.

On November 12, Brian had a quadruple heart by-pass operation, performed by top surgeon Alan Kerr, at Auckland's Greenlane Hospital.

A diet book he had heard about on the radio in hospital, became a vital part of his life; he was convinced it would prevent him having another heart attack. He ate only organic products and tried to persuade his family and friends to do the same. Phillip and Tim went along with him for a while, and they started growing vegetables in the garden. Phillip had to admit going on the diet made him feel good, even more energetic, but it didn't last long. When Brian and Pat went on holiday a few months later, he and Tim took the opportunity to tuck into meat. But the vegan lifestyle suited Brian and, as he would tell everyone he met, he was feeling fitter and fitter.

If Brian and Pat did have misgivings about New Zealand, the heart scare made their minds up. Quite honestly, it knocked the stuffing out of them. They started to say how much they missed England, particularly Pat's sister, Diane, and other members of the family they'd left behind. And, just after Christmas, they were so homesick they began talking seriously of selling up and returning to Cornwall.

His father's heart attack had brought the family even closer together, and the thought of being apart from them would have caused Phillip a great deal of anguish.

He was faced with a similar stay-or-go dilemma to the one he faced in 1981, while at the BBC.

To keep in touch with Britain, Phillip had been sending tapes of his Shazam! work to Peter Powell at the BBC. There seemed a lot of interest but nothing was definite. No concrete offers had been made. He could fly home and take his chances, but it would be a big gamble.

On the other hand, his career was developing spectacularly in New Zealand. He was not yet 22. Who knows what heights he would reach if he stayed.

In February, Phillip was told something that could make up his mind. Shazam! had proved so successful that TVNZ bosses were considering expanding it to a full hour. Phillip was overjoyed. An extra 30 minutes would open up so many exciting possibilities: he would be able to put on other big-name interviews, like the Elton John and Billy Idol specials that had pulled nearly 800,000 viewers.

Phillip's joy was short-lived. Before the end of February, the full hour idea was scrapped – and the cheeky smile that was his trademark vanished. He was so disenchanted, he was threatening to go home to England with or without the promise of work.

In the end, he didn't. With his Shazam! contract coming up for renewal in March, he had to make a decision one way or the other.

And, despite his parent's eagerness to leave, he decided to sign the contract to present Shazam! for another year.

# 8

# Love Fades Away

Romance may possibly have played a part in his decision. For Phillip and Marika were still together, going to concerts and parties, sharing holidays, and spending relaxing weekends at each other's homes.

That New Zealand autumn, the relationship was getting serious: Phillip had even started calling Marika's parents mum and dad and would insist on dropping in on her Russian grandmother who had also fallen for Phillip's charm and caring personality. Marika, in turn, was envious of Phillip's female admirers, particularly at the parties and official functions they went to.

Marika's mother said: "Everyone loved Phillip. He was a little idol and Marika didn't find it easy coping with the adoration he received. But he was faithful to her, and Marika knew it.

"Actually, Phillip wasn't a mad social partygoer. As a celebrity, he went to functions because he was expected to be seen, but he made sure he avoided parties at the weekend. That time was precious to him and he loved spending it with Marika and his family and us. My husband and I treated him just as a son."

It is clear that, as far as Mrs Tautz was concerned, Phillip was her ideal son-in-law. He was warm. He was kind. He was successful. And he thought the world of her daughter. Who could ask for more? Indeed, he was a very caring young man, with a novel way of doing things. For Marika's 21st birthday, for instance, he gave her a little box, containing just a bar of soap and watched, in amusement, as she tried to look and sound grateful. Then laughing, he gave her another box, wrapped the same way, saying: "No, this is your real present." Inside was a gorgeous silver bracelet.

Phillip was in love with Marika, but whether marriage was on his mind at that stage is not clear. If it was, it had to take a back seat because, shortly after his 22nd birthday in April, he was given a wonderful opportunity to realise the ambition he had had since those days as a five-year-old in Trenance Infants: to be a radio disc jockey.

Ross Goodwin, the voice-over link man who had been so impressed with Phillip on his Shazam! debut, was now programme director at Hauraki Radio, a former pirate station.

Radio Hauraki had become one of Auckland's most respected stations, but it was losing listeners – particularly kids – to rival stations on the FM waveband, and Goodwin wanted to do something about it. He had seen Phillip attract 2,000 adoring kids when he made public appearances for TVNZ and thought: If he can win the kids on TV, he can win them on radio.

Goodwin put the idea to Hauraki boss John McCready, who was not impressed. "A Pommie voice like that?" he said, contemptuously. "Are you mad?"

When Goodwin said he wasn't, and made out a case for taking a gamble, McCready relented: "Well, you're the programme director – do it if you want."

The questions for Goodwin now were: would Phillip want to do a radio spot? And, if so, when should he do it?

Goodwin was keen for a Sunday breakfast show – to attract kids who didn't listen during the week, and who were too young to be sleeping off the effects of a wild Saturday night: Phillip was the ideal person to capture them. But would he be interested in working on a Sunday – and getting up at dawn to be on air at 6 a.m. ?

Not very confident, Goodwin contacted Phillip and put the idea to him. He tried to be as persuasive as he could, but he need not have bothered. "I'd love to do it," Phillip said, instantly. "When do you want me to start?"

Goodwin was flabbergasted. And delighted. It was not until later that Phillip told him he'd loved radio as a child and had wanted to be a disc jockey all his life. Phillip's wages were small. But it didn't matter. The money meant nothing to him. He was, at last, realising his life's ambition.

The Saturday night before his debut, he went to bed early and arrived at Radio Hauraki an hour early, tense and keyed-up and quietly excited.

To try to put him at ease, Goodwin went into some amateur dramatics. "God, I feel rough," he kept saying. "I had a heavy night. Thank God, this isn't television. No one will be able to tell."

He played on the idea one could get away with a lot on radio and Phillip shouldn't worry if he got a few words wrong. But Goodwin really had no need to be concerned: Phillip was raring to go.

"He was certainly nervous, but he controlled it," Goodwin remembers. "I could tell only by a slight tremor of his hand when he moved the microphone nearer. That first day went fine – no problem. After that Phillip was a joy to have around.

"He was so natural. He didn't have a huge ego because of his TV adulation – never came into the station, playing the big star. Some people make the big time and become super private and want to talk only to equally famous people. Others go beserk and party all night. But Phillip was neither. He remained level-headed and charming."

It was this down-to-earth approach that endeared him to other disc jockeys, who might have been expecting a prima donna, carried away with his success.

Hauraki's Drive Time presenter, John Sweetman, says: "Phillip arrived as something of a star, but you'd never have guessed it. Unlike other TV people, there were no limousines or rubbish like that. He was a success because his infectious personality and love of life came over on air. He knew he was good at what he did, but he was never arrogant about it, just confident.

"Socially, he could be an entertainer, but wasn't the type to dominate a situation or crave the spotlight all the time. He was just a really nice bloke."

Phillip was a big hit with his young listeners, too. Normally, a good disc jockey takes a year, maybe more, to establish himself, but Phillip was an instant success. Within just six months he had more than doubled the station's audience for the Sunday breakfast spot.

Not bad for a beginner. But then, Phillip had known as a kid he'd be good on radio!

Phillip, the boy born to be a disc jockey, with his rapidly-growing record collection

New Zealand is a difficult place to be famous: the public expect TV and movie stars to be accessible, just like them. If someone is seen driving a limousine, people are likely to sneer, 'Who do you think *you* are,' rather than appreciate it as a symbol of success.

Executives in the unsophisticated world of TVNZ in the mid-eighties had the same narrow-minded mentality. They did not not allow their TV stars to rise too high in case they became too powerful and started causing problems. If they looked like getting too big for their boots, something had to be done about it.

It was called The Tall Poppy Syndrome: once someone gets too high, cut them down.

It was unfair – and stupid. But it was a fact of television life. And, in June, 1984, Phillip suffered from it.

Someone somewhere within the Government-run station decided that he was getting too big: he was flitting from one TV programme to another, he was presenting live shows, he was even becoming a big name on radio. He was a star who was shooting up too high, too fast. And he had to be brought down to earth.

Phillip had, quite simply, become a victim of his own success.

What was actually said behind closed doors in Shazam's offices towards the end of June has never been revealed. What is certain is that Phillip and Peter Grattan, had such a major blow-up that Phillip felt he had no option but to resign. And on June 22, a statement was issued, confirming he was leaving.

The next day, the papers carried the story, quoting Phillip as saying that he was left "with sadness and a sour taste in my mouth." He was disappointed for all his fans, but it would take "a lot of soul-searching" for him to change his mind and go back.

The soul search must have done the trick because, just three days later – after a showdown meeting with Peter and children's programme chief Huntly Elliot – Phillip did, indeed, change his mind and was reinstated. Peter put on file all the 100 hopefuls who had applied for the job and told the Press: "Phillip has become an integral part of Shazam! and it would have been hard to imagine the show without him."

For Phillip, it was hard to imagine life without Marika. The previous Christmas, he had given her a promise ring as a symbol of his love. And now, with his immediate future settled, he decided she was the girl he wanted to marry.

He took her to Parnell where they had shared that first lunch, and, as romantically as he could, popped the question.

Whether Marika suspected what was coming is not clear. Certainly she did not pretend she needed time to think about it.

She just said No.

And the rejection left Phillip devastated.

He was not the type of person to make an offer of marriage lightly, and Marika's reaction – possibly her manner, too – killed the relationship for him then and there.

In less than a year, he had been torn apart by the death of a dear young friend and the near-death of his father, and he found it hard to handle the anguish of another emotional trauma. He didn't want to see Marika again. And at work, he refused to speak to her, or even look at her: the hurt burned too deeply inside him.

His reaction upset Marika. She would go home and cry to her mother that Phillip was treating her as if she wasn't there.

"It was understandable from Phillip's point of view," Miriam Tautz says today. "I wouldn't like to say that Marika broke his heart, but I know he was deeply hurt. He was only 22 and very tender and vulnerable. He was very much in love with Marika and utterly devastated that she turned down his proposal. She felt she was too young to consider marriage, and just said No. I know she would have done it in the right way, but it doesn't stop the hurt. Marika was hurt, too, of course, but being so young, she probably didn't appreciate how Phillip felt. He wasn't the type to go around proposing to someone lightly.

"It was all terribly sad that it ended the way it did. I still feel sad today.

"When they broke up, Marika's grandmother would say, 'Why didn't Marika marry Phillip?' And I'd say, 'Mother, we have no say in these things.'

"Of course, I would have been happy for Marika to have married Phillip. Any mother would have wanted him as a son-in-law. He was just so delightful – an exceptional young man.

"Marika has never said she regrets her decision. But she will always have a soft spot for Phillip, because he was the first man she fell in love with."

At the studio, the break-up was soon common knowledge, but Phillip kept his hurt hidden from his colleagues. With his family about to fly back to England, he was having to cope with the prospect of "flatting and starving" on his own, and he wanted to get on with his career, not bother people with his personal problems.

So, over the next few months, he threw himself into work – and there was lots of it. Apart from Shazam!, he was now a resident judge on Starquest, co-host of a video phone-in show, as well as a radio DJ. To make life even more hectic, Peter Grattan decided to record Shazam! on Sundays, too, which meant Phillip had a tiring day ahead of him after getting up at 4 a.m. to prepare for his three-hour spot on Hauraki. On top of all this, he had his fan mail: he was receiving up to 50 letters a week, and he answered every one personally – even the abusive ones!

He would never forget Marika. But, as Auckland basked in glorious sunshine that November, the pain of their parting had eased and Phillip was ripe for romance once more.

It came in the petite shape of a ballerina named Fenella Bathfield.

# 9

# Farewell to Fame

Phillip met Fenella at the New Zealand Music Awards on Monday, November 12. The country's top entertainers and most powerful music and media people were in the audience at the Michael Fowler Centre, in Wellington. But Phillip, who was hosting the 90-minute live TV broadcast, had eyes only for Fenella, who danced in one of the stage acts between presentations.

And when they were introduced at a backstage party after the show Fenella fell for him, too.

She later told her mother, Adrianne Bathfield: "Oh, mummy, I've met Phillip Schofield. He's really lovely."

Adrianne was more than a little surprised. Phillip was not the archetypal muscular Kiwi rugby player and she'd heard young people refer to him as "that wimp Phillip Schofield."

She says today: "Even Fenella and my other daughter, Vanessa, who watched Shazam! from time to time, felt he was wimpy. A lot of kids expect men to be big and brawny, but Phillip was gentle and emotional. Fenella found him charming and easy to get on with, too. She was bowled over by him."

Adrianne was pleased for Fenella. She had lots of male admirers, from all around the world, but she sensed her daughter had a lot more enthusiasm for Phillip. She was "blown away" by his personality.

When Fenella took Phillip home, Adrianne found him charming, too. "I fell for him immediately," she admits. "He had a charisma that makes him stick out from the rest. But I found

Phillip a deep-thinking person who, basically, wants to know how everything ticks. That's a wonderful approach to life."

At the start of their relationship, Fenella was based with her ballet company in Wellington, nearly 300 miles from Auckland, so it was difficult for Phillip to see her as much as he would have liked. But they spoke on the telephone a lot, and when Fenella came home, Phillip did not want to be anywhere but with her.

He was in love. Madly, hopelessly in love. He did not talk freely about Fenella, or his feelings, but it was an open secret at work.

"He didn't come down to earth for days after the Awards," says work colleague Louise Jones. "He just went Boom, and fell in love. I remember him being totally distracted for more than a lunch hour! He just wanted to be with Fenella all the time. Like the song says, 'Love is the drug' – you can't get enough. Fenella was definitely the big one in Phillip's life.

"When he returned from Wellington he said he'd met someone he really liked. He was too much of a gentleman to reveal much. He just said she was a ballerina and very cute. But everyone in the Shazam! offices knew what was going on in one another's lives and we could tell it was full turboing love. Everyone was just pleased for him, including Peter Grattan. He was very supportive, just as long as the relationship didn't distract Phillip from what needed to be done for the show."

News of the romance did not take long to get round Radio Hauraki, either.

"They were a really hot item – always kissing and cuddling whenever they were together," says DJ John Sweetman. "I didn't think Fenella had much of a personality, but Phillip did, and when they were together, he would make her act nicely. In turn, she added a touch of glamour to him. They fitted perfectly."

The more Phillip saw of Fenella, the closer he got to her family, much to Adrianne's delight.

"He used to call me his New Zealand mum," she remembers with deep affection. "I loved him for that. And he loved me, too, I hope.

"All Fenella's boyfriends were lovely lads, but Phillip had that special factor that made him different. I became very fond of him because he was one of those young men who had all the qualities I would have loved in a son of my own.

"He has lots of imagination and tremendous drive. And, of course, he can hit a note. Fenella would tell me he loved Barbra Streisand's voice and would sing her songs as they drove along in his car. One day, she said: 'Mummy, if Phil's not going to be a TV presenter, he will be a pop star'."

Less gifted folk will be relieved to learn that, according to Adrianne, Phillip is hugely nervous, despite his super-confident persona. "He was always chewing his fingers," she says. "My other daughter, Vanessa, was just the same and whenever Fenella and I caught them chewing, we'd tease them and tell them to sit on their hands. With Phillip, it was just a sweet little thing about him – a sign that even he might be insecure in some ways. People see his polished performance on TV, but they don't see the nerves and tension and agony that goes into it. Phillip is the type who finds his confidence right at the eleventh hour."

After Christmas and at the beginning of 1985, it was decision time again for Phillip: should he go and try his luck in England, or should he stay and capitalise on his success and growing popularity.

Certainly his decision the previous March to stay had paid off. He had become one of New Zealand's biggest TV names, and, thanks to hosting the music awards, he was known by millions of adults now, as well as children.

He was established in a career that possibly – just possibly – knew no bounds. If he left, he would be throwing all those possibilities away. And for what? Back in England, Peter Powell was setting himself up as a showbusiness manager and told Phillip the promises of work were sounding hopeful. But that's all they were – promises. He could be faced with months out of work, and he knew how awful that could be. If he stayed in New Zealand, though, what was he going to do? He enjoyed Shazam! and he adored those Sunday morning radio spots, sitting in his small studio watching the sun rise over the gorgeous harbour the Maoris named Sparkling Waters. But did he want to still be doing that in, say, five years when he would be coming up to 30? To be brutally honest, did he want to continue to be a big fish in a little pool?

It seemed there were two ways of looking at his future. He could consider those prestigious music awards as the peak of a short-lived, but highly successful, career and leave the country with his fame and popularity intact. Or he could stay on and try to emulate that success in another area. Against that, however, was the danger of not being allowed to move on. Hadn't he been warned that he was now pigeon-holed as a children's presenter and switching to adult TV would be difficult, if not impossible?

In those early days of 1985, all the possibilities and options and hopes and fears swam around in Phillip's ambitious mind and, all the time, making a decison more difficult, was his love for his family he missed so much, and Fenella.

In the end, the family bond that had been tied even tighter by his father's brush with death, won easily over everything else. Phillip did feel he loved Fenella, but he loved his family more, and now they were back in England, that was where, deep down, he truly wanted to be, too.

Going back without anything lined up was a massive risk to take. But Phillip's deep family loyalty left him in no doubt that it was a risk worth taking. After all, he had given up everything before.

TVNZ colleague Fritha Goodman says: "He was sad to leave, because he had some good friends in TV. Here, people take you for what you are and we weren't especially impressed or unimpressed by Phillip's fame. We simply liked *him* and he liked that. He was torn about leaving because he liked New Zealand and the people. But he loved his family very deeply, and he did think he'd be frustrated sooner or later at not being able to move on easily to adult TV. It was definitely his commitment to his family that made him go."

Adrianne Bathfield freely admits she told Phillip he would be foolish to stay for Fenella's sake. "I wouldn't have wished my daughter on anyone at that stage," she says. "Their relationship was one of those lovely romances that can happen when you're young, but they both had so much happening in their lives at that time.

"Phillip was very fond of Fenella, though, and had mixed feelings about leaving her. I told him he was silly, and that he must go back because there was nothing in New Zealand for his talent. Eventually, he did choose to go. And we all had a tearful goodbye at the airport."

On January 30, a newspaper confirmed that Phillip Schofield was leaving Shazam! and returning to England.

In April, Phillip drew up at Auckland airport, where just three and a half years before, he had arrived, exhausted by the long flight, but excited at what lay ahead of him.

Saying farewell after all that had happened would have been an emotional moment for him.

He had arrived in the country, a raw teenager with little but hope and ambition to drive him on; and he was leaving as a household name, his radio dream partly fulfilled and general broadcasting talent recognised.

New Zealand was the place where he been given a chance to show what he could do, and he had grabbed it.

It was a place where he had fallen in love, not once but twice, and had experienced the pain of rejection.

It was where a dear young friend had died in the springtime of her life.

And it was where his love and strength and will had breathed back life into the father he adored.

He had so much to thank the country for and so much to remember it by. But now it was time to get back to Britain, where he truly belonged, and see what awaited him there.

Who knew what other dreams he might fulfil.

# 10

# Gordon's First Squeak

Phillip arrived back in Britain with just £800 to his name, but bags of optimism. He was, after all, an established TV presenter with more than three years' experience. And he had hosted New Zealand's premier music event live across the nation. Surely, it would all count for something in his second assault on the BBC.

Peter Powell was optimistic, too. Now concentrating more on showbiz management, he was enthusiastic about Phillip's future, particularly when he saw more videos of his work on Shazam! and heard the tapes of his Radio Hauraki broadcasts. Peter sent copies of both to his friends and contacts in TV and radio, and was not in the least surprised when one producer, Peter Hamilton, showed an immediate interest.

Hamilton, who had produced Peter in The Oxford Roadshow, on BBC2, in the early eighties, was looking for a new presenter to give the programme – newly-named No Limits – a fresh look for its Friday evening slot. And, after seeing the Shazam! footage, he felt Phillip had potential. The two met for lunch in Notting Hill Gate, West London, and Hamilton remembers it well, because he inadvertantly put Phillip down.

"He was proud about his work in Shazam! and told me the show had 800,000 viewers," says Peter. "Thinking in terms of BBC figures, I thought that was low, and said something like, 'Oh, hard luck – don't worry about it.' I had no idea that 800,000 was great

*The success story continues on Page 89*

HAPPY FAMILY: Phillip with his mother, father and brother, Tim.

STAGE HANDS: Phillip (second from right) with Ian Jago (far right), and other friends take a break during rehearsals for a school theatrical production.

LITTLE CHARMER: Phillip (left) and Louise Tucker (sitting) and her sister, Nici, while rehearsing for Cinderella at Phillip's house.

SMILE, PLEASE: Phillip, at 20, neatly groomed to appear on Shazam!

STARMAKER: Peter Grattan and his young protege plan the success of Shazam!

STAR AND STRIPES: The new presenter faces the camera with confidence.

LOVE STORY: Phillip and Marika, the girl he fell for when she joined the Shazam! production team. Phillip asked her to marry him, but she said no.

PUPPET LOVE: Phillip (right) with his best friend, Gordon the Gopher.

DYNAMIC DUO: Phillip, in fancy dress, and Jason Donovan on stage together.

CROWD PLEASER: Rolling into town with the BBC Radio 1 Roadshow.

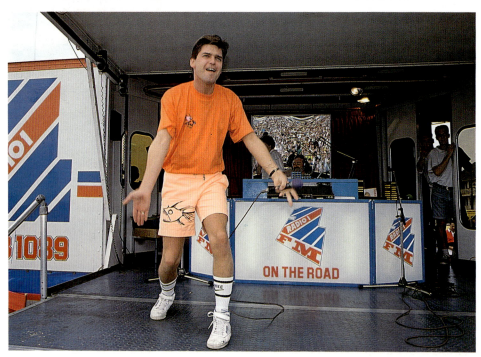

SMASH HIT: Phillip dressed to the nines at the BRITS awards ceremony.

RIDING HIGH: Phillip on top of the world with Going Live.

STAR GUEST: Neighbours actor Stefan Dennis joins Phillip and Sarah Greene on TV

UP BEAT: Phillip gives a deafening drum roll on the Roadshow.

DRESSED TO KILL: Phillip and new girlfriend Stephanie with Sarah Greene and Mike Smith, get into gangster gear for the premiere of the movie Bugsy.

BOSOM BUDDIES: Manager Russ Lindsay and wife, Caron joking with Phillip.

FITTING SCENE: Jason hands over his Amazing coat to new boy Phillip.

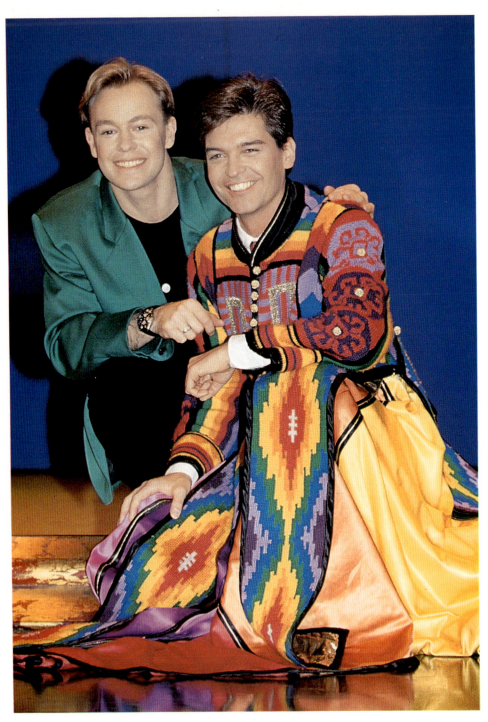

GOOD LUCK MATE: The coat fits and Jason wishes Phillip all the best.

for New Zealand. Poor Phillip must have been deflated by my reaction, but took it very well.

"He was ambitious to be a BBC presenter. But although I was impressed by the high standard of his Shazam! work, I had to tell him he wasn't right for my show. We had 200 people in the studio audience, with live bands and lots of other things happening, and I needed someone with a huge amount of character – someone quite spiky. I told Phillip he was too clean for the job – I actually used those words. He was disappointed, but seemed to understand."

The young man who eventually got the job would also go on to become a children's TV favourite. He was Timmy Mallett.

The No Limits rejection was the beginning of several worrying months out of work for Phillip. He could not persuade anyone to take him on and it brought back bad memories of those first few frustrating months in New Zealand when he feared he would never find a breakthrough.

This time, however, there were some huge differences. In Auckland, he had had his family, a lovely garden and warm sunshine to help him cope with his disappointment. But, now, he was broke, sharing a tiny London flat with a friend, and his parents were 300 miles away in their new home in Cornwall.

The only work Phillip did that summer of 1985 was televised interviews with stars at the Wembley Live Aid concert, which were later shown on Shazam! in New Zealand. Working for TVNZ on a casual basis only seemed to highlight Phillip's fears. Had he made a mistake leaving the comparative security of Auckland? he wondered. Should he not have stayed on there and tried for a job in England, while still a big-name working presenter?

There were times when he would have thought the heavy doors to the wonderful world of broadcasting – particularly the BBC – were closed tighter than ever. But the fighting spirit and self-belief that had carried him through difficult times before was unshakeable, and, shortly after moving into an East Finchley flat with his dad's cousin, Phillip's amazing resilience paid off: he was taken on as a short-term relief presenter with a new satellite TV company called Sky Channel. And within weeks of leaving there, he got another holiday relief job as a disc jockey with Capital Radio, based in Euston, North West London.

The job was for only 14 weeks and at the dead of night. But, at least, it was in broadcasting in the heart of the city, and the station had arguably the biggest listening audience outside the BBC. It was a step in the right direction.

After all those fruitless months, Phillip began to feel, for the first time, that his luck was changing.

Luck was not changing that August, however, for the BBC's promotions editor, Pat Hubbard. He had been given the go-ahead to introduce children's programmes with live links by a young presenter, instead of the stuffy, pre-recorded adult voice. But he had interviewed more than 50 young people without finding one who was suitable, and time was pressing on. Pat had just three weeks before the new-style live links were to be given their chance.

He needed a fresh, young presenter, bright enough to talk to nine million children without a script; someone clever enough to talk to the children like a big brother, as if he was sitting on the carpet watching the television with them, not merely introducing the programmes.

But no one, it seemed, fitted the bill. In desperation, Pat started auditioning actors from the Grange Hill TV soap series, because they, at least, had camera experience. But still he could not find anyone with the qualities he was looking for. Finally, with time running out, Pat plumped for a young lad from local radio. He was not right, by any means, but he was the best of a relatively poor bunch.

And then, late one afternoon, Pat's secretary, Dee, told him she had "a really nice boy" on the phone who wanted an audition.

And Pat's luck changed.

The "nice boy" was Phillip Schofield. And, thanks to that secretary, he got in to see Pat and had his audition.

Today, Pat recalls: "I was a bit tired with it all and said to Dee, 'For Christ's sake, tell him I've finished auditioning'. But Dee said to me, 'He sounds a really nice boy. He says he can come in and see you today.'

"When I shook my head, she said: 'Go on, Pat, see the boy. Give him a chance'.

"I've always been soft hearted. And, in the back of my mind, I wasn't 100 per cent happy with the boy I had chosen, so I thought, why not? Something inside my head said that, in showbiz, there is always the chance of the right person coming along.

"Phillip arrived at my big fifth floor office in jeans and a very washed-out T-shirt. He sat in an armchair in front of my desk, looking very frightened. I remember thinking that he looked in need of work.

"He told me about his time on Shazam! and I noticed he had picked up a slight New Zealand accent. Then he said he'd been working on Capital Radio. We chatted for about half an hour and there was something about him, apart from his good looks, that made me decide to give him a chance.

"I booked him to do a camera test the next day. I got him to read out what was on television that afternoon, as if he was giving a run-down for the viewers. He had no idea what would be on the list, or what the programmes were about, so I told him to make some up if he wanted.

"In the middle of the list, he told the imaginary viewers: 'Then we have Zorro … ' and drew the letter 'Z' in the air as if he had a sword in his hand.

"As soon as I saw him do that I got a gut feeling he was just what I was looking for. He had that special spark and the ability to project amazing niceness. I had to go for him. Most of the other kids had tried to put on the voice of a typical BBC announcer, but Phillip was so much more natural. I was very relieved and gave him the job."

Until now, most of Phillip's fans and the majority of magazine and newspaper journalists, thought that he got that live link job because his Shazam! show reel had been passed to BBC executives in London after he failed to get the No Limits job. But it was his own phone call to Pat Hubbard that did it – and the secretary, who sensed he had something special.

How Phillip knew that Hubbard was looking for a children's linkman is not clear. What is certain is that Phillip's telephone call late that August afternoon was the most crucial of his career.

It was a call that prised open those heavy BBC doors and gave him the chance he had been longing for.

The irony would not have been lost on Phillip. After six months unemployed in Auckland, he had arrived out of the blue to solve Peter Grattan's problem. Now, after another six months' out of work, he had cured another TV boss's headache.

There was a big difference, of course. In New Zealand, he appeared in front of thousands of children in a pre-recorded show. In Britain, he would be chatting to NINE MILLION – live and without one word of script.

September 9, 1985. A big day for the BBC – the day the live link format was introduced. And the BBC's big wigs were watching very closely. Some of them felt it simply would not work; others feared they were letting young people loose on the air without any real control. Understandably, everyone connected with the links was nervous. Everyone, that is, except Phillip.

Tim Mackay-Robinson, then an assistant producer on the afternoon link, recalls: "We were all thinking, this is never going to work, but Phillip was super confident. He kept saying we were going to get through it, no problem. And we did."

Not without Phillip having to cope with a mini crisis, however.

One of Phillip's links was at the end of Blue Peter: he had to chat about something for 10 or 15 seconds and smoothly introduce the next programme. In normal circumstances, no problem. But that day, as bad luck would have it, Blue Peter finished early. Not a few seconds early – TWO full MINUTES early. The show's credits finished, and there was Phillip's face filling the screen ... with his audience of millions watching and waiting to see what was coming next.

Phillip could have sat there, frozen, struck dumb with panic. He could have lapsed into some stupid senseless rambling that would have left him red-faced and killed off his British TV career before it got started.

As it was, he calmly, and almost without thinking, drew on the experience of those three years on TVNZ and sailed effortlessly through the two minutes, ending with a smooth link into the following programme.

Most of the watching BBC chiefs were impressed. The lad was only 23, but he had coped with a mini crisis like a true, veteran professional.

But not everyone thought that way. One high-ranking executive hated what he saw that afternoon and later sneered at Pat Hubbard: "Get that cringey wimp off the television immediately."

Thankfully, Pat ignored that command. The new link format was his responsibility and, unless something went drastically wrong, he made the decisions.

Today, he says: "Naturally, I stuck up for Phillip and the concept of the live link. I was happy with the way it went and relieved nothing had gone wrong technically. Phillip was not especially good, but I knew he would improve with time."

What worried Phillip was that he might not be given time. He was on only a two-week contract and Hubbard's bosses were still so unsure of the live links they kept everyone in the dark about whether that they would be allowed to continue.

One thing the BBC hierarchy were left in no doubt about was Phillip's growing popularity.

His young audience quickly warmed to Phillip's natural, relaxed manner. He earned himself another two-week contract. Then one for a month. Finally, his bosses had no option, but to extend it to six months. He was so perfect for the job that the original idea of bringing in two presenters every few weeks was long forgotten.

Phillip broadcast from a continuity suite he dubbed The Broom Cupboard, at Television Centre. He seemed at home there: everything had to be ad-lib. It never fazed Phillip. If anything went wrong, he coped brilliantly. If something off-camera distracted him, Phillip would make fun of the interruption by pretending it was an imaginary character – such as Sid the Caretaker, for example – making the noise. The kids loved it.

Phillip had always found that humour was the best way out of an awkward situation – and it was one flash of wit that led to the birth of Phillip's hugely-popular sidekick, Gordon the Gopher.

That Christmas, Phillip's Auntie Diane had given him a joke present she had picked up in a market in Cornwall – a long-limbed, furry, yellow puppet that made a squeak when you squeezed inside its mouth. Phillip was amused by the puppet, and he brought it into the BBC after Christmas. During one of his links he said simply: "I think my family are taking my job a little too seriously – look what my auntie got me for Christmas!"

He held up the toy and laughed. Then, he put it down on the table. As far as he was concerned, that was the beginning and the end of the furry animal's TV career.

Later that day, however, Tim Mackay-Robinson, who was known for his slightly zany sense of humour, decided to have some fun at Phillip's expense. As Phillip completed a link, Tim put his arm up the puppet and pushed it into view on the camera, making it squeak loudly.

"It wasn't planned or rehearsed – it was just something I did off the cuff when I saw the puppet lying on the desk," Tim recalls. "I just started being disruptive and knocking things off the desk. I found it quite funny because Phillip was trying to speak to the camera and I was trying to put him off.

"Those few seconds were the very humble beginnings of Gordon the Gopher. It was all completely spontaneous. When the link was over, Phillip and I suddenly twigged that there was great comic potential in that badly-behaved puppet, and a couple of days later, I made it knock over the Christmas tree.

"The routine seemed to gather pace from there and I played an increasing part in the puppet's character. Someone suggested calling it Gopher, then Phillip came up with Gordon, because it sounded good, like Donald Duck and Mickey Mouse.

"I started to crouch under the desk with my arm inside Gordon and pass things to Phillip and bite his arm. I would make Gordon misbehave and be very naughty because I knew that Phillip would always react well. It was the unpredictability that was so funny. If we rehearsed anything it would have fallen flat.

"There were days when we got up to so much mischief that we would cry with laughter when the lights went down and we closed the show. The thought of the stupid nonsense we had just done on live TV was hilarious. It was the first time anything like that had been done. It was anarchy. The more chaos the better.

"At times, Phillip would be biting his lip just to get through without cracking up. It was unbridled television and the funniest time of my career. I would catch Phillip out by squeaking Gordon at the worst possible moment and start biting him – a bit like Rod Hull and Emu. It was manic and I would be under the desk with tears in my eyes. We would just muck around and Phillip was bright and quick enough to react.

"Gordon caught the children's imagination extremely quickly. In a matter of weeks the letters started coming in and before we knew what had hit us there were two sack loads in the office and kids were sending in jumpers they had knitted for Gordon. The success ran away with us and, to be honest, none of us expected just how big he would become. Gordon was one of those things no one could have planned. Phillip and I stumbled on him by fluke."

In those early days, drastic surgery was performed on Gordon in the TV Centre office to make him more cute and easier to handle. First, his arms were cut off and shortened, then his legs. A caring secretary kindly put the new Gordon back together on her sewing machine at home.

Today, one of the original dismembered arms is still tied to a talk-back mike at the BBC!

The fun on the screen was working for the young viewers, but some high-ranking executives were still not convinced it was a good thing. Ironically, it took a tragedy to make them appreciate Phillip's qualities of communication with children.

On Tuesday, January 28, 1986 the American space shuttle, Challenger exploded seconds after take off, killing the crew of seven. Childrens' programmes were continually interrupted by news flashes and then it was back to Phillip. Instead of carrying on with the normal zany behaviour as if he had not seen the terrible news, Phillip talked to his young viewers about the disaster, and reassured them in such a responsible and mature manner that it was noticed and applauded by his doubting superiors.

That Tuesday was the day Phillip proved himself. From then on, his efforts and talent were appreciated at all levels within the BBC, not just the presentation department. It was the day his future as a BBC broadcaster seemed assured.

Gordon the Gopher became an integral part of Phillip's "performance". Their joint popularity soared. And so did the fan mail. He had not forgotten all those childhood hours he had spent writing letters himself, and he had promised his young viewers he would reply personally to every letter he received.

In the beginning, he coped easily; there were only a dozen or so letters a day. But now, as he and Gordon went from strength to strength into the New Year, the letters poured in by the hundred. Phillip was still determined to reply personally, however, and things got out of hand.

Producer Ian Stubbs remembers: "Once the letters started arriving by the sackload it got ridiculous. Phillip would sit in the office writing out replies whenever he got a spare moment during the day, then take whatever was left in the sack home with him.

"The sack would be half full with at least 300 letters in it. Phillip didn't want to send off just a signed photo – he wanted to write a proper reply because he said he had experienced what it was like writing in as a child.

"He would come in the next day looking shattered because he had been up half the night writing to kids. It got so bad that the long hours and strain started affecting his work; he wasn't looking as fresh as he should on camera. One day I said to him: 'Look, Phillip, you're going to have to let me bring someone in to help.' He had to admit it was the only answer, so I brought in some clerical staff to deal with the fan mail."

One letter that gave him an extra special thrill was from Gerry Green, the schoolteacher he had "stonewalled" in that classroom chat about his career. Someone told her he was on television, so she wrote, congratulating him on proving her wrong. Phillip was so touched, he read out the letter during one of his links.

Around that time, one of his primary school teachers, Joyce Cane, thought it a good idea to ask Phillip to come back to the school and judge a talent competition. She wrote, not expecting to hear from him, but Phillip replied by return of post, saying he would be delighted.

"He came in the afternoon with his mum and dad, and an aunt, who had children here," Joyce recalls. "Phillip judged the contest – and everyone won, of course. Afterwards, I saw him chatting to some children, who wanted his autograph, and it gave me an idea. I asked him if he would mind signing autographs for 10p each and we'd donate the money to our Guide Dogs for the Blind appeal.

"But Phillip said No. Instead, he signed his autograph for everyone for nothing, then wrote out a personal cheque for the appeal. He was lovely. He hadn't changed a bit."

In that summer of 1986, he went back to the senior school to officially start a charity race. Naturally, his former teachers wanted to know what he was going to do next and Phillip admitted he had his sights set on Saturday morning live TV.

And he revealed he wanted it so badly he was going to turn down an offer to join a nationally famous TV programme.

The offer, from Blue Peter producer Biddy Baxter came in September, after Phillip had done a nine-week stint, presenting Take Two, a children's version of the viewers' write-in programme, Points of View.

The legendary Mrs Baxter was so impressed with Phillip she told him he could join her programme without even having an audition. She approached him personally because she knew the presentation department would not let their star go willingly. She was right. When they heard she was trying to poach him, they refused to release Phillip from his contract.

It didn't matter; Phillip turned the Blue Peter offer down. That may sound a bold decision and, in many respects, it was. But Phillip was shrewd enough to know that the show can do more damage than good to careers because, as other presenters have discovered to their cost, it is extremely difficult to shake off its name tag.

He wanted something far more challenging. And he knew just what it was.

# 11

# Sacked by the Boss!

As Phillip approached his 25th birthday on April 1, he was able to look back on the two years since his return from New Zealand, with immense pleasure and satisfaction. He had stuck it out in the rain, when no one seemed to recognise his talent, and now he was enjoying the sunshine of success.

He had waited and waited for his chance and, like Shazam!, he had taken it. The camera still loved him. And Britain's kids, like those down under, did, too. Almost by public demand, Phillip – with Gordon, naturally – was given a guest slot on Mike Read's Saturday Superstore that summer. They were an instant success there, too.

It seemed the only way for the dynamic duo to go now was UP.

And then, on August 21, 1987, the impossible happened.

The boss of the BBC, Michael Grade, gave both of them the sack. There, on screen, in front of millions of adoring fans, Phillip was summoned by Mr Grade and given his marching orders; told to take the next three years off and go and work in the post room.

It was unthinkable. It was unbearable. And, of course, it was untrue.

Phillip's contract was not being renewed because he was going on to better and bigger things. He was going to move to that Saturday morning spot he had dreamed about.

He was Going Live!

And the fact that Mr Grade chose to have some fun himself on air proved that he viewed Phillip as one of the BBC's brightest new stars.

Going Live! was a new Saturday morning version of Superstore, which aimed to mix pop, fashion, quizzes and phone-ins. And the producers had just the young lady to co-host the show with Phillip. Like him, she was bright and bubbly, with a natural on-screen style. Her name was Sarah Greene.

For both of them, it was the biggest break of their careers. But if Phillip was thrilled that he'd been chosen to front the new high-profile programme, he did not show it. He told the Press that it was all down to luck. He had simply been in the right place at the right time.

It was the same modesty that had captivated thousands of youngsters in New Zealand. And it would take him into the hearts of millions in Britain; and not only the very young children who had watched him link those early evening programmes. His good looks, it appeared, were now attracting an older fan and, much to Phillip's astonishment, he was voted Britain's Most Eligible Bachelor in a magazine poll. The attention was flattering, he said, but if the girls who voted saw him first thing in the morning after a night out they might think differently.

At that time, there was one young woman who, according to gossip-hungry journalists, might have witnessed those bleary eyes and stubbled chin on occasions. She was Caron Keating, daughter of Radio 2 disc jockey and presenter Gloria Hunniford, and talk of her affair with Phillip was buzzing round the BBC.

Just how deep the love affair was, only Phillip and Caron can say. Certainly they were not rushing into print on the subject. Phillip simply refused to confirm or deny they were lovers.

Whoever Phillip *was* seeing, he went out of his way to keep it secret. He had made a deal with himself that no matter how famous he became, he would try to keep his private life just that – private. It would be difficult, because he was, to a large extent, public property; but he had seen other stars' lives wrecked by being too open and revealing, and he was not going to let it happen to him.

Anyway, far more important than romance at the moment was that daunting debut – live! – in front of eight or nine million young viewers in a new show all the BBC big wigs would be watching carefully.

You would have thought, with all that Shazam! experience and the live New Zealand Music Awards broadcast behind him, that Phillip would have been relaxed, perhaps even looking forward to that first Going Live! show. But Fenella Bathfield's mum was right. He was a nervous type, who, somehow dragged up his courage and confidence at the eleventh hour.

And the Friday night before the September 26 transmission, he didn't sleep a wink.

He need not have worried. His personality blended perfectly with Sarah's, and the new format show sparkled with a freshness and topicality the kids adored. Within months, it was THE weekend children's programme and Phillip's popularity – and Gordon's, of course – continued to soar.

With such a demanding show to front, Phillip could have been forgiven for taking things easy; could have been excused for thinking that, at 25, he had come far enough, done enough, to satisfy that burning ambition. But the workaholic in Phillip kept telling him that there was a lot more time left to do other things while he was not preparing for Going Live!

The more he thought about this, the more he thought about radio. The childhood dream was still there: the little kid who'd told his teachers all those years ago that, one day, he would be speaking on BBC radio, still wanted to do it.

And in the early part of 1988 he told his Going Live! colleagues so. He talked about his yearning more and more, and he sounded so keen, so determined, that one of the team, Annabel Giles, bet him £100 that he would be playing records on Radio One before the year was out.

It was a bet he would be delighted to lose, and he knew his management were doing their best for him. But there seemed nothing in the pipeline that summer, as Phillip planned to take a two-month break, including a couple of weeks in New Zealand.

Phillip had a great time down under, looking up old friends – including Fenella – and flew back to England, tanned and refreshed and eager to get back to work.

He was surprised to find one of his managers, Russ Lindsay, at the airport waiting to greet him.

Russ was grinning broadly. He had some great news.

Phillip had lost his £100 bet.

He had been given a spot on Radio One, starting in October.

The following month, Phillip went on air with his own radio show. It was Sunday, October 2 – a date Phillip would never forget. The day that burning childhood ambition, the hope that most of his schoolteachers thought merely a dream, was finally realised.

The following year, 1989, was when it all came together for Phillip; when all the self-belief and patience and dedication and hard work began to pay off in terms of money and national recognition.

It began in February when he picked up the TV Times award for Best Children's Presenter. Then, sales of Gordon the Gopher toys and other merchandising rocketed so much Phillip was able to buy a beautiful four-bedroomed house in West London. He had commandeered the first-ever Gordon, and, now, it took pride of place on a shelf in his new home. It was a fitting tribute to the puppet, because it helped pay for the house: a toy firm struck a deal with Phillip to sell a modified version of Gordon and sales ran into hundreds of thousands.

In November, a poll of 20,000 young people, carried out by two magazines published by Barclays Bank, voted him the year's most outstanding and popular television personality. Then, to cap an amazing year, the now very powerful Capital Radio tried to entice him away from the BBC by offering to almost double his salary.

Phillip was flattered but politely declined. The Press were probably wrong that he was nearly a millionaire, but it is certain money was not Phillip's motivation. The job was what interested him; he loved what he was doing, and where he was doing it. More to the point, he was the golden boy at the BBC with a golden future ahead of him. Now that he had finally made it to the place he'd dreamed about, he was hardly likely to sell himself out for cash. That just wasn't his style.

The little boy with that burning ambition had grown into a young man who was achieving all he'd said he would. But, despite his soaring popularity, he was still as unassuming and fun-loving as ever, with his feet firmly on the ground. He knew where he had come from, what he had been, and he knew about failure and rejection as much as success. He was still that likeable Newquay kid at heart.

That's why, at the end of that smashing year of 1989, Phillip would have looked back on one moment with more pride, more satisfaction and certainly more joy than he'd felt at any other time. It was when he went back to Newquay in August with the Radio One Roadshow and saw the thousands of pop-crazy kids on the beach where he'd sat himself, a star-struck 11-year-old, in the summer of 1973. Looking at the front row of adoring youngsters, Phillip had glanced at the spot he had chosen to sit that hot July afternoon and felt a lump in his throat.

He had left the town with all the hope of youth, and returned a hero.

And the thought made him want to cry.

If 1989 was the year Phillip's whiter-than-white profile established him even more firmly as the young people's favourite, then 1990 was the year he seemed to do his best to muddy that squeaky-clean image.

Uncharacteristically, he told a tabloid newspaper about his current relationship with Fenella Bathfield – and landed himself in an embarrassing position when the story was picked up in New

Zealand.

Phillip was quoted as saying he and Fenella had a most bizarre relationship. They didn't see each other for a long time, but when they did it was like "a smouldering fire," and they crammed everything into three weeks. "It's fun that feels naughty," the paper claimed he said.

Fenella, who was now a radio DJ, too, was peeved when an Auckland reporter rang her to ask what she thought of Phillip's remarks, not least because she had a live-in lover, who didn't appreciate Phillip claiming to be still in Fenella's life.

She threw cold water on the "smouldering fire" quote, saying: "I'm going to ring him and tell him to stop making these remarks – they're getting very boring.

"Certainly I was very close to Phillip, but now I've met someone else, he is a thing of the past."

The mini tiff made headlines in both countries – and finally killed off a relationship that had been fading ever since Phillip had left New Zealand.

Romance was almost certainly closer to home for Phillip at that time. Two years before, children's TV presenter Andy Crane, a close friend of Phillip's, had introduced him to a lovely 24-year-old BBC secretary named Stephanie Lowe at a party. They had hit it off immediately and, it seemed, they were seeing more and more of each other.

The Fenella row was nothing to the storm Phillip caused a few months later at a Radio One Roadshow in Weston-super-Mare, Somerset.

Matt Goss, of the pop band Bros, was singing to 40,000 Brosettes on the beach when several boys in the crowd started pelting him with eggs. Phillip, who was the guest DJ, looked on, not knowing what to do. But, then, one of the eggs hit a woman in a wheelchair in the front row and Phillip blew his top. He rushed on to the stage and yelled at the culprits: "I don't normally use language like this, but you're a bunch of w******." And he appealed to them to behave.

His outburst was heard by the crowd, and the egg-throwers in particular, but fortunately did not go out over the air. Afterwards, he was unrepentant, and the BBC backed him up officially, saying: "Phillip doesn't regret using the word – in the heat of the moment it was entirely justified."

The newspapers had a field day. Mister Clean using a dirty word! Shock! Horror!

In October, Phillip seemed happy to shatter his image altogether when the producers of a new travel series, Schofield's Europe, suggested he undressed totally for a scene in a Finnish sauna.

At first, Phillip refused point blank, saying he didn't want everyone seeing what his "private bits" looked like. But he could not see the sense in going into a sauna with his clothes on, so he agreed to strip, provided the cameraman respected his modesty.

In the end, the scene was filmed in the best possible taste, with the briefest glimpse of Phillip's bare bottom as he climbed on and off a massage table. Far from being embarrassed, he thought it a good giggle.

Phillip was still being secretive about his love life. If he was seeing Stephanie, he wasn't saying anything. Work came before everything. He lived for TV and radio, thriving on a punishing seven-days-a-week schedule.

Whenever he was asked about girlfriends, he said that he had no time for them. Unlike in the past, when he had put his heart and soul into a relationship, there now was not room in his life, he said. In the spring of 1991, he was even wondering, sadly, if he had forgotten how to fall in love. He just hoped that when "the time comes for someone to open the door to my heart, the lock hasn't rusted."

Whether Stephanie Lowe was trying to open the door to his heart, he was not publicly admitting. But it does seem certain, in view of what was to emerge later, that she WAS. For, only a matter of months later, she was rumoured to have moved in with Phillip at his Chiswick home.

Steady girlfriend or not, Phillip was not lacking in offers for romance – or blatant lust. His appeal to the opposite sex had spread with the weekly screening of Schofield's Europe and, because the show went out at 8.05 p.m., it meant that adults now watched him, too. He was getting around 2,000 letters a week, but now, mothers were writing to him as well as their daughters. And when it came to sexy suggestions, Phillip had to admit that the mums had the more creative imaginations.

With his national popularity soaring daily, Phillip was in great demand to host live TV awards' ceremonies. One he particularly liked doing – the Stars Organisation for Spastics' Charity awards – passed without any controversial or unforeseen incident, but at another, on October 27, Phillip was knocked to the ground while speaking to camera, and had to be helped to safety.

It happened at the Smash Hits pop magazine's Pollwinners Party at London's Docklands Arena, after a performance by Carter the Unstoppable Sex Machine. The eccentric pop band were cut off 26 seconds early while miming their hit After The Waterhead. Guitarist Leslie Carter, known as Fruitbat, immediately kicked his microphone stand into the orchestra and a colleague knocked over their speaker monitors.

As the band left the stage, Phillip was said to have quipped something like: "That was original." Fruitbat turned back and launched himself at Phillip, bringing him to the ground with a flying rugby tackle. Phillip vanished from the TV screen for several seconds as he fought off the pop star. Minders rushed to separate them and Phillip quickly went before the BBC1 cameras again, shaken, but unhurt. Typically, he refused to criticise the band or its leader, saying they were merely over-enthusiastic.

That autumn, Phillip had reason to be bubbling with excitement himself. Apart from Going Live! his Radio One Sunday spot and all the one-offs and personal appearances that went with the territory, he had completed another six-part series of Schofield's Europe, which promised to help, still further, his transition into adult TV – the move that would have been so hard for him to make in New Zealand.

He had been to Amsterdam and toured the notorious Red Light district – the equivalent of London's Soho. He had made three wishes with a witch in Barcelona, flooded a brewery in Prague and dipped into sewers of Vienna, where the classic movie, The Third Man, was filmed. He had been attacked by a seabird while golfing in Iceland. And he had been to the world's only Circumcision Palace, in Turkey, where young boys had the delicate operation in a mass ceremony. They were exciting times, indeed.

And as if the workload was not enough, Phillip had also made a pilot for a brand new, totally different and original series, aimed at ALL viewers. It was called TV's Greatest Hits and was all about classic programmes of the past.

He adored Going Live! It was arguably the biggest break of his career – bigger, perhaps, than even Shazam! – and he loved the pressure of a long, live show. But Phillip had always been a forward thinker, and when he looked ahead he was slightly worried that he might be trapped in Going Live! that he would still be presenting it when he would be too old. In a few months, he would be 30; not old in general terms, but old enough for a children's idol. To a teenager, someone in their thirties could sound ancient. He wanted to avoid that awful label, "oldest teenager in town."

He certainly did not want to be presenting the show sitting in a comfortable armchair, wearing a thick woolly jumper, in ten years or so.

It was not an immediate worry. He had no intention of saying goodbye to Going Live! and his millions of fans, for two, maybe three, years. It was just something he knew he had to be aware of; a niggling fear at the back of his mind that would not go away.

And then, one day in October, he got a call from Peter Powell, saying that Andrew Lloyd-Webber had a proposition for him.

And Phillip knew that he stood on the threshold of a dream opportunity that could change his life for ever.

# 12

# You're Brill, Phil

Phillip's management got a call from Andrew Lloyd-Webber because his West End show, Joseph and The Amazing Technicolour Dreamcoat, needed a replacement for the starring role. Jason Donovan had been playing Joseph virtually every night since June and needed a rest: Lloyd-Webber wanted someone to step in for six weeks while the former Neighbours TV star took a holiday.

Certain young actors, including another ex-Neighbours' heartthrob, Craig McLachlan, came to mind, but Lloyd-Webber had a strong feeling that Phillip could be the ideal choice. He had the looks. He had the personality. He had the charisma. And, more important, he had a huge young following – vital for what was essentially a childrens' show.

Lloyd-Webber believed that certain people are "Joseph" types and felt that Phillip most definitely was. He had been impressed with Phillip when he had been interviewed on Going Live! and had a hunch he could be great in the stage role. The composer knew very little about Phillip, however, so he went in by the back door and talked to people who worked with him on the programme. Everyone said the same: Phillip was a true professional who took everything he did very seriously. If he said he could deliver, he would.

That did it for Lloyd-Webber. From that moment, he had Phillip in his sights for one of the most enviable opportunities in West End musical history.

What the composer did not know was: Did Phillip have a good voice? And, if he had, would he be able to sing in front of 2,300 people, six nights a week, on the most famous theatrical stage in the world – the awesome London Palladium?

There was only one way for Lloyd-Webber to find out: he would invite Phillip to have an audition and hear for himself. After that, he and his Really Useful Company, which produced the show, would decide whether or not to take a chance on him.

When Phillip was told of Lloyd-Webber's interest, he laughed. Convinced someone was trying to wind him up, he told Peter Powell to ring The Really Useful Company back and ask to speak to the person who, supposedly, made the call. When he learned the call – and the offer – was for real, a mixture of emotions flowed through Phillip.

He was flattered, of course. And excited. But he was nervous, too. For a young man whose public vocal performances were limited to singing A-Ha and Duran Duran hits in his Shazam! office or serenading girlfriends with Barbra Streisand songs in his car, the prospect of singing to the legendary creator of Jesus Christ Superstar, Cats, Phantom of the Opera and Starlight Express was daunting, if not plain terrifying.

But, after speaking with his mum and dad, and other close friends, Phillip had little hesitation in agreeing with Peter Powell that he should consider very seriously going for the audition: it was too big an opportunity to let slip. His voice may not impress Lloyd-Webber, and he may not get the role. But there was nothing lost in trying. And if he did get it, six nights a week for six weeks at the London Palladium would be wonderful experience. Who knows where that could lead to?

It was all terribly tempting, but the professional in Phillip prevented him from merely saying: "Yes, I'll give it a go." He told Lloyd-Webber that he was thrilled even to be considered for the part, but would want to have some voice coaching to see if he could manage it. He did not want to waste anyone's time.

The lessons went well and, by the time of the audition, in late

October, Phillip's excitement had calmed down into a quiet confidence. Okay, he may not get the role, but, at least, he would not embarrass himself – or Lloyd-Webber, come to that. As with everything else he had done in his life, he would give it his best shot. He could do no more.

The audition, at the Lyric Theatre, in Hammersmith, West London, was like a classic Hollywood movie scene of a Broadway audition, with Mr Lloyd-Webber and his executives sitting in the silence of the stalls, looking up at Phillip, waiting to hear what he could do.

And it was then, standing alone on the empty stage, that all Phillip's confidence vanished and he felt more frightened than at any time in his professional life.

Someone started playing a piano. Then someone else, down there below him, called out, asking if he could hear it from where he stood. Phillip went to reply, but couldn't find his voice: he was so terrified, he'd dried up. A few seconds later, he managed to clear his throat and shouted out that he could hear. And he added apologetically: "I'm extremely nervous."

He was offered some kind words of encouragement to calm him down, then he was asked to sing a couple of lines from Any Dream Will Do, the show's hit song, which Jason Donovan had taken to the top of the pop charts.

Phillip took a deep breath and broke into song. Despite his nerves, his voice was strong and clear and in perfect tune. The pianist kept playing and Phillip, his adrenalin flowing, kept singing. Before he knew it, he had got to the end of the song and was being asked to sing another. That went well, too, and he left the theatre reasonably pleased.

It had been a terrifying ordeal. But even more nerve-racking, in a way, was the next day. Having conquered his fear and got through the audition, he desperately wanted to know what the great man thought. If he didn't think much of it, Phillip wanted to know as soon as possible. If the answer was No, he wanted to be put out of his misery and get over his disappointment quickly.

Phillip had got the impression Lloyd-Webber might ring him – or Peter Powell – the next day. Every time the phone rang, he hoped it would be him, saying he had got the part. But the morning passed without contact. In the afternoon, Phillip and some friends were glued to the TV, for the England-Australia rugby union World Cup Final, and every time the phone rang, his pals all leaped up and screamed, thinking it was the great composer. Phillip tried hard to be nonchalant, but his stomach was churning; he wanted so much to hear, one way or the other.

That all-important phone call was made early the following morning to Peter Powell, who was naturally, excited. But he resisted the temptation to phone Phillip. He had sensational news – and he wanted to deliver it personally. He wanted to see Phillip's face when he told him he was going to be a West End star – in the hottest musical in town!

He drove to Chiswick, and as soon as Phillip saw the car he knew he'd got the part. With a live radio show that afternoon, Peter would not arrive on the doorstep with bad news!

Phillip, of course, was beside himself with joy that Andrew Lloyd-Webber was "very impressed" by his vocal skills, and equally pleased that Jason Donovan could not think of anyone better to take over his role for six weeks.

If he were honest, however, Phillip had to admit that taking the part was a risk. He was an established TV presenter, not a stage vocalist, and he could fall flat on his face; perhaps humiliate himself and set his TV career back years.

But he was in no doubt at all that Joseph was a spectacular opportunity for him, and that it was a risk worth taking. So did his friend and Going Live! co-host, Sarah Greene. She encouraged him to go for it from the moment he was offered the part.

Another side of Phillip was unconcerned that certain critics might be rubbing their hands with glee at the prospect of knocking him off his pedestal the moment he sang off key. Given his background, his long, uphill battle to get where he was, this is hardly surprising. He had got his life and career into perspective years before. He loved what he did and the fame that went with it, but he was under no illusions that his work was what he'd describe as outrageously important; it wasn't as if he were a brain surgeon!

He had never taken anything on that he thought he couldn't do. But if he had made a mistake and it did all go wrong – so what?

Everything was signed and sealed the next day, Monday, with only family and friends in on the secret. Then the newspapers were told. And, not surprisingly, they went crazy.

Suddenly everyone wanted to know more about the cheeky-faced children's favourite. From being merely a popular TV presenter, Phillip was thrust into the national spotlight where everything about him, it seemed, was of media interest.

The Newquay kid, who'd set his young sights on just the BBC all those years ago, now seemed to have the whole country at his feet.

The day the Press broke the news on the latest West End sensation was Tuesday, November 5 – Guy Fawkes Day. Phillip had just 68 days to prepare himself for his momentous first night on the Palladium stage. Sixty eight days in which to wonder whether his portrayal of Joseph would rocket him to stardom, as it had Jason Donovan ... or whether it would fizzle out into a damp squib and be savaged by the critics as a rare mistake by the millionaire with the musical Midas touch.

Professional as ever, Phillip made three important decisions after accepting the role. One was to take voice coaching every day from mid-morning to early evening. Another was to go on a low-fat, high-carbohydrate diet to lose weight for the part. And the third was to kick his 20-a-day cigarette habit. The six-week stint was going to be tough. He would be working it round his TV and radio shows. He would have to be super fit.

By the time, Monday, January 13 came round, Phillip WAS. He had lost more than a stone, and his work-outs in the gym had built muscle and toned up his body. The lack of nicotine had made his breathing easier. He looked good. And felt it.

All he would have liked, waiting to walk on to the famous Palladium stage, was the butterflies in his tummy to calm down!

He had sung with the orchestra for the first time, the previous day, and again that Monday afternoon, and everything had gone well; everyone was pleased. But now he was to do it for real – in front of 2,300 people, including newspaper journalists who might be wanting to see him flop.

And the prospect was awesome.

One of the authors of this book, Robin, 26, was lucky enough to be there that Monday. Here is his story:

*It was an unforgettable experience.*

*The tremendous excitement hit me as I walked along Great Marlborough Street, which runs alongside the Palladium, and heard the chants of "Phillip ... Phillip" rising from dozens of devoted fans, spilling into the road outside the stage door.*

*None seemed to have tickets, but they had braved the January chill anyway to wish their heart-throb good luck. Holding photographs and teen magazines, they chanted his name in the hope that he would emerge from the stage door to acknowledge them.*

*But, for Phillip it was not a time for autographs. Deep inside the theatre, in the No.1 dressing room that had been used by international stars down the years, he was changing into a white cotton tunic and having the final adjustments made to his long, flowing "Joseph" wig.*

*The countdown to the biggest night of his life was quickening. His moment of truth was getting nearer.*

*I walked round to the main entrance in Argyll Street. There was a buzz of excitement here, too, albeit less raucous. But something in the atmosphere was different to the night, months before, when I'd seen Jason Donovan open in Joseph, and I could not put my finger on it.*

*It was only when I took my seat in a box, to the left of the Royal Circle, that I realised what the difference was.*

*With Jason, his acting ability and voice were well known. Nobody expected anything less than a good professional, polished perfor-*

mance. That June night, I and the rest of the audience were able to relax and enjoy the show, knowing that Jason would not make a fool of himself.

But with Phillip it was not the same. He was a TV presenter, not an established actor, and nobody outside the people who'd hired him knew if he could sing or act. Unlike with Jason, there was every possibility that Phillip would dry up or freeze and turn the show, and the whole evening, into an embarrassing flop.

It was THAT, the terrifying uncertainty of it all, that was worrying me, and the rest of the 2,300 audience; we were all worrying for Phillip, nervous for him, and our nerves – mixed with the usual tension of a first night – gave the atmosphere a unique edge, making it quite different to anything I'd ever experienced.

It was as if we had all gathered to watch a dangerous stunt that could go horribly wrong, and there was nothing any of us could do, except watch and hope.

The front row, on the left of the Royal Circle, was reserved for Phillip's family and close friends, and girlfriend Stephanie Lowe. In the stalls, were Andrew Lloyd-Webber and his wife, Mike Smith and Sarah Greene and other celebrities. Like the rest of us, they waited nervously.

Then, the lights went down. The music started. And the show began.

A line of schoolgirls in pretty dresses filed through an aisle at the side of the stalls, walked on to the stage and sat cross-legged around an up-right wooden chair. A narrator began reading the story of a "dreamer called Joseph" and, slowly, a thick fog from dry ice filled the stage behind the children. A shadow started to move in the background. It was Phillip. High on a hydraulic platform, he made a slow arc through the air and out of the thickness of the clouds to the middle of the stage. The moment the audience realised who the shadow was, an almighty roar filled the theatre – an amazing highly-charged cheer, spiced with piercing screams from fans high in the upper circle, and it sent goose bumps down my arms and a shudder along my spine.

I stared at Phillip on the platform, in his white tunic and wig. He seemed frozen, like a statue, his eyes fixed straight ahead. The only movement was from his jaw as he swallowed anxiously and rolled his tongue to wet his mouth, left dry through fear. He was in the air only a few seconds, but it must have felt longer; he must have thought he would never find his voice.

The platform settled on the stage and Phillip stepped out, to deafening cheers and applause. The opening bars of Any Dream Will Do rose from the orchestra pit, and he started to sing and the noise quietened into a stunned silence.

Phillip had cut deep through the nerves and adrenalin and found his voice. He walked centre stage to the children and sang with them, their sweet voices complimenting his in the chorus.

Minutes later, at the end of the song, the roar from the audience surpassed even the greeting he had got as that shadow in the mist.

It was a stunning performance. From the moment he finished that opening number, you could see Phillip begin to enjoy himself. True, he looked rigid and awkward in places, as if he was trying desperately to remember where to stand and what to do next. But his voice was powerful and in tune and he got the laughs in the right places.

The weeks in the gym had paid off: his physique, when he wore a loin cloth, looked good and the definition of his stomach and chest were starting to take shape.

The audience willed him through every scene. They could only guess what kind of nerve it must take to come from the familiar surroundings of a TV studio to the terrifying vulnerability of the world's most famous theatre. They wanted him to be good; they wanted him to triumph.

The ovation he got at the end is something he will never forget. Neither will I. Everyone was on their feet, cheering as he skipped through the cast to take his bow.

It was a moving ovation that, not only bought out the goose bumps again, but also made the eyes fill. Typically, Phillip did not come out, showing off with arrogant, "I showed you" salutes. There was no need for extravagant waving; it is not in his nature anyway. Instead, he *looked out to the audience almost stunned, with just an enormous smile.*

*I saw a girl in the front row of the stalls holding up a white sign. It said: "You're Brill, Phil." Her hero saw it. And beamed at her.*

*And then, for the grand finale, Phillip put on the Dreamcoat again and stepped onto another hydraulic lift that took him high above the stalls to the front of the Royal Circle.*

*The crowd were going even madder. For a moment, Phillip seemed oblivious to them. There, just feet in front of him, to his right, was his mum and dad and Tim and Stephanie. He looked at them, at the dad he had brought back to life, now punching the air with pride, and they were all on their feet, smiling, with tears in their eyes.*

*Phillip looked at them. He gently grinned. Then, in an intimate gesture, meant only for them, he slightly raised his right arm from the hip and gave them the most subtle thumbs up.*

*He'd done it.*

*And he'd done it for them.*

# The Dream Goes On

That triumphant January night ended with the most amazing grand finale. Unknown to the audience, Andrew Lloyd-Webber had been so impressed with Phillip's performance that he went back-stage during the interval and offered him the role for six months when Jason Donovan finished in May. High on the euphoria of the first half of the show, Phillip grabbed the chance, and took the stage for the second half, knowing his whole life was about to change dramatically.

After the final curtain, when the audience had gone, Lloyd-Webber led Phillip on to that now empty stage and held his arm in the air, like a referee at the end of a boxing match, and told dumbfounded newsmen that the West End had discovered a fabulous new star.

The fairytale that could match many a Hollywood script sent the newspapers crazy the next morning. They raved about Phillip's performance and praised his courage for gambling his reputation on the role. Their excitement had an immediate effect: the Palladium box office – which had been quiet, with people waiting to see how Phillip fared – was flooded with requests for tickets and, by the end of the day, more than £100,000 had been taken in advance bookings.

For once, Phillip seemed at a loss for words to describe how he felt. He had spent nine weeks building himself up for the big opening night, but nothing could have prepared him for the reaction of the Press. What was more incredible, however, were the decisions he had had to make, following Lloyd-Webber's sensational offer. His life had been turned upside down, he said; he was being swept along in a totally different and new direction. For the past 12 hours, he felt as if he had been living in Disneyland!

Phillip's six-week run was a staggering success. He had only one problem. After the first week, he thought his voice had gone for good. He panicked, thinking of the ridicule of the headline: "The Man Who Could Only Sing For A Week." But, fortunately, the Palladium doctor diagnosed only tonsillitis and Phillip was able to carry on.

After Jason stepped back into the role on February 25, Phillip's life returned to relative normality, with Going Live! and the launch of his new programme, TV's Greatest Hits. Reluctantly, he made a decision to take an indefinite break from his Radio One Sunday show once he returned to Joseph.

And to make sure he was super fit for the role, he made plans to continue his gruelling fitness schedule, pumping up his muscles and running for miles on a machine to build up his stamina. Phillip had never been a sporty kid, and, before Joseph, he would have laughed at the thought of becoming a fitness fanatic. But he was a dedicated professional and was determined to be in top condition when he took the stage again.

He had been a little boy with a dream to speak on the radio. Swept along by an unshakeable self-belief, he had battled against the odds to fulfil it.

Now, he had gambled his career, and the reputation he had fought so hard for, on a West End starring role. And he had won again.

It is a spectacular, breath-taking success story that the Newquay kid, for all his burning ambition, could not have imagined in all his wildest, most amazing, technicolour dreams.

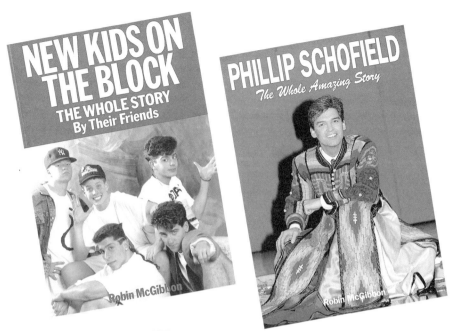

## *Two amazing stories by the same author*

★ If you've enjoyed reading Phillip's success story, buy the book for a friend today – it makes the perfect gift. Fill in the coupon over the page and we'll send the book to you by return.
***AND WE'LL PAY THE POSTAGE!***
Send just £4.50

★ If you haven't read New Kids on the Block – The Whole Story, By Their Friends, you MUST. Donnie Wahlberg and the rest of the band have said it's brilliant and hundreds of thousands of kids around the world have raved about it.
Send just £4.50

**TURN OVER FOR COUPON**

Send to:
# ROBIN McGIBBON
80 Crystal Palace Park Road, London SE26 6UN

If you want to buy the Phillip Schofield book, fill in the appropriate space and leave the New Kids space blank, and vice versa. If you want both books, fill in **BOTH** spaces.

## PLEASE RUSH ME

............copy/copies of Phillip Schofield – The Whole Amazing Story. Price £4.50 per book (includes postage).

............copy/copies of The New Kids on the Block – The Whole Story, By Their Friends. Price £4.50 per book.

I enclose cheque/postal order made payable to Robin McGibbon. Price £4.50 per book (includes postage).

Name _____

Address _____

_____

_____

_____ Postcode _____